Centre for Educational Research and Innovation (CERI)

EDUCATION, URBAN DEVELOPMENT AND LOCAL INITIATIVES

ORGANISATION FOR ECONOMIC CO-OPERATION AND DEVELOPMENT

Pursuant to article 1 of the Convention signed in Paris on 14th December, 1960, and which came into force on 30th September, 1961, the Organisation for Economic Co-operation and Development (OECD) shall promote policies designed:

- to achieve the highest sustainable economic growth and employment and a rising standard of living in Member countries, while maintaining financial stability, and thus to contribute to the development of the world economy;
- to contribute to sound economic expansion in Member as well as non-member countries in the process of economic development; and
- to contribute to the expansion of world trade on a multilateral, non-discriminatory basis in accordance with international obligations.

The Signatories of the Convention on the OECD are Austria, Belgium, Canada, Denmark, France, the Federal Republic of Germany, Greece, Iceland, Ireland, Italy, Luxembourg, the Netherlands, Norway, Portugal, Spain, Sweden, Switzerland, Turkey, the United Kingdom and the United States. The following countries acceded subsequently to this Convention (the dates are those on which the instruments of accession were deposited): Japan (28th April, 1964), Finland (28th January, 1969), Australia (7th June, 1971) and New Zealand (29th May, 1973).

The Socialist Federal Republic of Yugoslavia takes part in certain work of the OECD (agreement of 28th October, 1961).

The Centre for Educational Research and Innovation was created in June 1968 by the Council of the Organisation for Economic Co-operation and Development for an initial period of three years, with the help of grants from the Ford Foundation and the Royal Dutch Shell Group of Companies. In May 1971, the Council decided that the Centre should continue its work for a period of five years as from 1st January, 1972. In July 1976, and in July 1981, it extended this mandate for further five year periods, 1977-1981 and 1982-86.

The main objectives of the Centre are as follows:

- *to promote and support the development of research activities in education and undertake such research activities where appropriate;*
- *to promote and support pilot experiments with a view to introducing and testing innovations in the educational system;*
- *to promote the development of co-operation between Member countries in the field of educational research and innovation.*

The Centre functions within the Organisation for Economic Co-operation and Development in accordance with the decisions of the Council of the Organisation, under the authority of the Secretary-General. It is supervised by a Governing Board composed of one national expert in its field of competence from each of the countries participating in its programme of work.

Publié en français sous le titre :

L'ENSEIGNEMENT,
LE DÉVELOPPEMENT URBAIN
ET LES INITIATIVES LOCALES

© OECD, 1983
Application for permission to reproduce or translate
all or part of this publication should be made to:
Director of Information, OECD
2, rue André-Pascal, 75775 PARIS CEDEX 16, France.

Whereas national development has long been a principal concern of the OECD Member governments, regional development to even out the adverse effects of certain national policies and historic and geographical difficulties has been a more recent interest. Increasingly, however, that too has been seen to be too broad and to need complementing by a more locally targeted approach. In regional development, education has had a significant role as an earlier OECD report (<u>Education and Regional Development</u>) showed; but it has become increasingly apparent that this role should be extended to embrace local development activities also - particularly in the rich societies where, in spite of massive improvements in the living standards and cultural opportunities, areas of disadvantage - and indeed outright poverty - continue to exist.

<u>Preliminary analysis shows that while such poverty certainly exists in the more remote rural areas, the major poor communities live in the hearts of cities</u> in the more developed OECD countries and on the urban periphery in Mediterranean ones. Millions are living in such poor areas, receiving inadequate welfare services and very little in the way of educational opportunities. This has been aggravated by the recent increase in unemployment and downturn in economic fortunes - the inner cities, in particular, being the hardest hit. In some conurbations the redistribution of population, planned with good intentions in better times, has created poor periphery areas facing much the same problems as their inner-city counterparts elsewhere. It was in these circumstances, persisting in so many Member countries, that the CERI Governing Board initiated an enquiry to bring together promising practices and policies in such a way as would clarify and utilise the role of education in the development of local communities.

Starting in 1978, the work was carried out on two fronts - rural and urban. The report on the first was published in 1981 (<u>Rural Education in Urbanized Nations: Issues and Innovations</u>, Westview Press, Boulder, Colorado); the urban setting is covered by the present report by Professor Jane Marceau, formerly of the CERI Secretariat. This is based on accounts of innovative practices in Member countries and the documentation for the Concluding Conference on Education and Urban Development, held in Venice in April 1980.

           J. R. Gass
           Director, Centre for Educational
           Research and Innovation

Also available

MANAGING URBAN CHANGE:
Vol. I: Policies and Finance (May 1983)
(97 83 02 1) ISBN 92-64-12442-X 150 pages   £8.50   US$17.00   F85.00

Vol. II: The Role of Government (November 1983)
(97 83 04 1) ISBN 92-64-12478-0 114 pages   £5.00   US$10.00   F50.00

EDUCATION AND REGIONAL DEVELOPMENT:
Vol. I: General Report (October 1979)
(91 79 05 1) ISBN 92-64-11945-0 92 pages   £2.60   US$5.50   F22.00

Vol. II: Technical Reports. "Document" Series (February 1980)
(91 80 01 3) ISBN 92-64-01996-0 462 pages, bilingual   £8.90   US$20.00   F80.00

Prices charged at the OECD Publications Office.

THE OECD CATALOGUE OF PUBLICATIONS and supplements will be sent free of charge on request addressed either to OECD Publications Office, 2, rue André-Pascal, 75775 PARIS CEDEX 16, or to the OECD Sales Agent in your country.

CONTENTS

Introduction 7

PART ONE: PROBLEMS AND POLICIES 10

  A. The Urban Background 10

     1. Employment: reduction both in quantity and
        quality of opportunity 12
     2. Housing, environment and population mix 14

  B. The Consequences for Education 15

  C. Urban Policies and Practices: The Need for a New
     Approach 19

     1. Models and misdirections: the French urban
        planning experience 19
     2. Development with the people, by the people,
        for the people: Building up from below 25

PART TWO: EDUCATION AND THE PRE-CONDITIONS FOR DEVELOPMENT 32

  A. Attitudes, Values, Interests 32

     1. Learning the locality: local studies and
        environmental education 34
     2. Territorial education: An Italian experiment ... 41
     3. Discovering entrepreneurship: "Micro-societies" 44

  B. Interacting with the Local Community: An Active
     Approach to Individual Learning and Community
     Improvement 50

     1. Community involvement programmes 50
     2. Housing, environment and welfare improvement:
        Programmes for inner-city youth 55
     3. Housing rehabilitation.......................... 56

PART THREE: EDUCATION'S ROLE IN ECONOMIC DEVELOPMENT 59

    A. Secondary Education and Enterprise 60

        1. School-based youth enterprises 60
        2. Youth in-school enterprises in Hartford
           (G. Richmond) 63
        3. School-business consulting activities 66

    B. Linking Work and Education for Development 67

        1. Youth enterprise and training outside school ... 67
        2. From employment to education to employment 69

    C. The College as a Community Development Resource 70

        1. Improvement of the quality of life 70
        2. Business and entrepreneurial training 72
        3. Links between colleges and development planners . 74
        4. Reaching the disadvantaged 74

    D. Linking the College with Local Enterprise
       (N. Falk) 75

        1. The problem of local economic development 76
        2. Existing college initiatives 78
        3. Improving the links between college and
           community 85

PART FOUR: CONCLUSIONS. NOT EDUCATION OR DEVELOPMENT –
          EDUCATION FOR DEVELOPMENT 90

    A. Education-Development: Forging an Effective
       Alliance 93

        1. Curriculum 93
        2. Teaching methods and the ordering of the
           learning process 94
        3. Staffing courses 95

    B. Issues for Analysis and Themes for Further Work 96

    C. Epilogue 99

Bibliography 101

Introduction

THE NEED FOR ANALYSIS BEFORE ACTION

The ELD project started by recognising that, in present economic circumstances, the solution to the problems of urban poverty cannot be found in individual movement to areas of greater prosperity. In most of the places with which we are concerned there is a mismatch between individually held skills and opportunities available (both locally and nationally) and, to be blunt, there are simply not enough jobs available anywhere. Much labour, then, is relatively immobile and is going to remain so, adults and young being tied in by many social and public policies that have created situations of poor public transport, excessive separation of affordable housing and possible employment, and a totally inadequate information network. What is more, past policies of encouraging home ownership and recent public housing policies contributed to the immobility and made the risks of moving elsewhere too great to be palatable. The only effective way, therefore, to improve the conditions and life chances of many people is to improve the areas in which they live.

Such improvement, as the project showed, has many components. Principal perhaps, is economic development, both in the sense of the creation of new additional jobs and more generally of better jobs. On the social side must come improvement in living conditions in the disadvantaged area. This should include satisfactory provision of social services; access to appropriate educational institutions and non-formal training; enrichment through cultural and recreational facilities, adequate housing and physical environment, and, above all perhaps, a feeling by the people concerned that they count as individuals and families in the life of their area and their country.

This initial conviction that economic development is basic to increasing the long-term well-being of the community as a whole carried with it the corollary that justified the project's purpose, namely that education, in both its formal and non-formal variants, has a vital role to play in human resource development and, therefore, in economic development as well. At the local level education may be involved in development in two major kinds of way and these directed the course of the enquiry. First, both formal and non-formal education play an important role in creating the attitudes and skills necessary to improving local conditions.

Some are "social" skills in the broadest sense and involve abilities to cope with local agencies, leadership talents and organisational skills. Others are more technically-based competences and their possessors constitute a pool of qualified labour which may attract in outside employers, thus contributing to bettering local job opportunities. Yet others are entrepreneurial skills which may be used for job creation and for the organisation of efforts to improve local amenities and necessities such as housing. Second, the ways in which education and training are carried out may make a direct contribution to local development. The school or college itself is, of course, frequently a major employer of local people and a generator of income which encourages local commercial and even manufacturing activity. But beyond this, particular methods of teaching and learning may involve local people in the creation of new goods and the provision of new or improved services. Experiments being tried in this area in a number of OECD countries are cited in the body of this report.

Educational activities of many kinds may thus make both indirect and direct contributions to local development. They cannot, however, be fully effective on their own. A third line of enquiry therefore followed the proposition that successfully rejuvenating local communities requires that policy-makers and officials from both the development and educational sectors must work together. This would mean generation of arrangements that involve the different cycles and branches of the education system in the realisation of development plans. It would also mean that education and training personnel recognise the importance in the success of their efforts of involving their clients, whether pupil or adult student in the real development needs of their local communities. As the original ELD proposal pointed out, this collaboration has immediate benefits for both sides.

The need to disseminate success

Let there be no misunderstanding that the severity of urban problems, decreasing public resources, increasing unemployment and a deteriorating physical environment in which the ELD project was conceived, have gone unattended by national and local authorities. The need for priority to be given to improving conditions has been recognised in many OECD countries; but the initiatives taken involved a good deal of experimentation and it is particularly important that the successes so far achieved should be given due public recognition – not least to enable their repetition elsewhere. This function has been assumed by the ELD project in this, its final report, which brings together information about experiments and innovatory strategies currently being put into practice or planned for the immediate future in different Member nations. This is believed to be the most valuable contribution the OECD can make at this time, especially because there is no existing international forum, such as a journal, for the diffusion of information on practices in this complex field.

Sources of data

The report presents data gathered from numerous sources (as credited in the text) by the CERI Secretariat and information provided by participants for the Project's final meeting held in Venice in April 1980. This meeting, titled "Education, Urban Development and Local Initiatives" will be referred to several times in the report. It was co-sponsored by the Italian Ministry of Education and CERI, the participants being experts from all Member countries interested.

The data available to us at this stage are of necessity rather disparate and fragmentary and we have no special reports on the detailed workings of particular innovations or experiments. Country conditions and their educational and administrative arrangements also vary enormously. In spite of this, it became clear in the course of the research that the project had struck an area whose importance a number of countries were coming to appreciate. The Venice meeting showed that in spite of specific country differences, the project raised issues of interest to many. Even more important, many of the innovations described seem to be transferable to countries with very different educational organisations and philosophies. Everywhere there seemed to be places in which many, although of course not all, of the "promising practices" presented could be slotted with nothing but beneficial results to all concerned. Young and old in the deprived areas need their problems attended to now. As an American participant in the Venice meeting expressed it, the people are not a problem; the conditions in which they live are. A change in emphasis is called for; dealing with those conditions is a challenge, not a problem, and one to which everyone, not least the residents of those areas, has a contribution to make in responding positively and successfully. An important input to that contribution is helping all concerned to go more quickly by learning "what works".

Part One

PROBLEMS AND POLICIES

A. THE URBAN BACKGROUND(1)

According to a recent OECD report(2), urban residents constituted approximately 75 per cent of the total population of the OECD area in 1975. This proportion is still rising as urban areas have become major generators of employment, wealth, capital investment and foreign trade. Currently in the world nearly 2,000 million people live in cities; by the year 2000 this number will exceed 3,000 million.

Although in some Member countries there is a drop in the recent rate of urbanisation and in a few very large cities even an absolute drop in population, the importance of urban living in these countries is undeniable. While, on the one hand, cities generate jobs and wealth, on the other they are also major absorbers of public funds. They are the locus for the major share of social welfare provision for education and for the implementation of many major aspects of social policy. National policies must of necessity contain important urban referents. While, as a recent OECD report underlines, there is a renewal of public interest in rural areas (Sher, 1981), nevertheless - as we have just observed - three out of four inhabitants of OECD countries currently live in cities.

These sentences give some indication of the critical problem of urban areas in OECD Member states but they do not of themselves indicate the nature of or the reasons for the severe economic and social problems faced by many metropolitan zones. While "economic and social problems" are not as yet coterminous with "urban area",

---

(1) The OECD recently completed a programme of work on urban problems, which is summarised in "Urban Policies for the 1980s", OECD, Paris 1983 (available free)

(2) "Urban Statistics in OECD Countries", OECD, Paris 1983 (available free).

very many urban centres are increasingly faced with massive difficulties. These problems constitute the context of, and indicate the need for, the redirecting of education in deprived metropolitan areas - the theme of this project. The reasons for them, therefore, have to be spelt out.

The reasons for such crisis in many, once thriving, cities are complex: some are economic, some the result of the interaction of diverse social policies, notably housing and the provision and delivery of welfare systems; others have developed in the wake of more or less centralised physical planning and land use strategies, operated with a national or regional rather than a local perspective. The relative importance of each will vary from city to city and country to country and any particular configuration will be unique. However, in spite of this diversity, both of cause and result, there are a number of common threads.

First, economic changes and particularly the recession beginning in the early 1970s have altered both the economic climate in general and the markets for specific goods. Changing patterns of production have modified the location decisions of many industries and undermined the prospects of growth or even survival of others. As the locus of the preponderance of economic activity, urban areas have become especially vulnerable to recession with its attendant problems of unemployment and inflation, and to shifts in national and international policies with respect to trade and the use of natural resources.

More specifically, a number of sectoral changes have taken place and, linked to these, there has occurred a change in the location of the more dynamic economic activities. There have frequently been shifts in the regional distribution of growing industries - from the north-eastern areas of the United States, for instance, to the west and southern states. Sectoral changes also have selective urban impact. Pre-existing differences both between and within cities are made more visible by such changes. The symptoms of such structural adjustments are now serious in many major cities in OECD countries.

Another factor that has become increasingly apparent in recent years is the relationship between national economic prosperity and urban conditions. The recession has squeezed municipal revenue in many OECD countries mainly due to lower business activity and higher social welfare costs. At the same time, inflation has had a disproportionately high effect on labour-intensive municipal services and energy price increases tend to be felt more acutely in large cities, where, because of the mix of activities, per capita energy usage is highest.

The most general effect of recession, therefore, has been to reduce the income of large cities and hence threaten even further their often precarious financial viability. Not all cities, of course, are equally affected; but most urban areas nowadays have their pockets of particular disadvantage, with populations frequently, but by no means always, "minority" or immigrant. Their disadvantage lies particularly in three aspects of human existence: employment chances; housing and recreation facilities; and the availability of social welfare and education services. Let us look at these in the light of information gleaned in the course of the project.

1. Employment: reduction both in quantity and quality of opportunity

In very many countries employment possibilities within the inner city have significantly decreased as the cumulative effects of poor environment and high costs have forced both many middle-class families and many companies to the suburbs and many firms have "died".

In the decades of the 1960s and 70s, for example, employment in areas outside the 85 largest United States cities grew considerably (46 per cent) while employment in the central cities grew by only a small amount (16 per cent). The increase in suburban areas was more than three times the increase in central-city employment ("National Urban Policy Report of the President", quoted in Wolman and Mueller, 1979). The problem is again much more serious in the old industrial areas of the Northeast and Midwest than in the newly developing South and West. A similar situation can be found in Great Britain and in continental European cities such as Paris.

Where companies are concerned, the reasons for moving to the suburbs include a perceived shortage of skilled labour in the cities, especially their inner areas. This, of course, is part of a vicious circle, for the combination of poor job security, low income and limited job opportunities has already led to a persistent outflow of high quality management and skilled personnel and this, in turn, greatly impairs the capacity for the city to generate new companies. Finally, as important firms move out, those that have served them have to move, too, or stay jobless. The process of decentralisation of economic activity, then, is cumulative. Even after a recession ends, in toto less labour will be used in the cities than before.

In some British cities, including London, there has even been an absolute loss of employment. Over much of Europe a similar shift has been occurring and in spite of overall sub-urbanisation trends (in part due to migrations out from the city), there is still a mismatch in many areas between population and jobs available.

The problem, notably in Europe, is not restricted to the biggest conurbations. In some of the smaller European cities severe problems occur where traditional industries (which usually are very large employers) are in decline. Their demise affects not only their own workers but also many others through the closure or contraction of associated sub-contracting and supplying companies, and the diminution of commercial activity. Old industrial areas in Europe, such as the region of Limburg in Holland, the Ruhr in Germany, and Styria in Austria, as well as the north-west and north-east of England and the north-east of France, demand extensive efforts on the part of the public authorities and private interests and individuals to re-utilise existing skills and investments and create new ones.

Overall employment chances have thus much declined. Equally serious are the shifts in the type of employment that is available to inner city (or poorer periphery) populations. It is in manufacturing that the greatest loss of opportunity has occurred (see OECD Urban Statistics, 1983, p.19). In recent decades in the central areas of American cities, for example, manufacturing employment declined, while outside these areas it grew by just over a fifth.

The decline in manufacturing industries is particularly serious because it is such industries that mostly provide skilled and stable jobs. Their loss means that local urban adult populations contain skills they can no longer use while young people are offered only largely unskilled, unstable jobs in the tertiary sector. This problem is widespread across Europe's older areas. In Greater London, in the 1960s and 1970s, manufacturing jobs declined by almost a third. In Birmingham, too, in a five-year period between 1971 and 1976 such jobs declined 20 per cent. This represented a loss of 59,000 jobs of which 53,000 were in the inner city. Here it was the large employers, nine companies representing 45 per cent of Birmingham's manufacturing employment, who were the biggest contributors to the loss. In one year alone, 1976, they "accounted for a net loss of 7,500 jobs in the inner city with an associated flow-on effect to smaller suppliers and sub-contractors" (Mr. Shaylor, City Planning Officer for Birmingham, quoted in Arclight, July 1979). Mr. Shaylor went on to point out that replacement of the annual job loss in the city would in itself require the re-creation of 70 additional jobs every day, a task, as he said, "clearly beyond the scope of public authorities acting by themselves".

Unemployment in the crowded suburbs and outer barrios of expanding southern European cities frequently is no less acute, although due to different causes. Recent migrants, attracted by the lure of apparently easily obtainable jobs, in fact often find they are the first hit by any social economic crisis. These migrants, too, are often concentrated in unstable, often seasonal, industries such as building. They live often in makeshift housing, with minimal physical amenities and low standards of health and nutrition. While children find odd jobs, their school attendance is frequently poor and irregular and they are unlikely later to find any but the least skilled work.

While the consequences of both growth and decline are not always adverse, some areas are particularly hard hit. In most cities, some quartiers and neighbourhoods seem to bear the brunt of the mixture of social and economic problems and cultural and educational deprivation while others escape almost untouched.

Within these neighbourhoods, the worst-hit sections of the population are usually young people, frequently girls, and people belonging to regional or national minorities, whether immigrant or migrant. Youth unemployment there is, of course, extremely serious. Perhaps the worst hit are American cities but many cities in European Member countries and in Australia are also facing severe youth unemployment problems. In some places the situation is dramatic. Thus, in Atlanta in 1978, in one small neighbourhood with a population of three and a half thousand people, not one single youth aged between 16 and 19 was employed. Over a large area of the same city, the youth unemployment rate was nearly 70 per cent. In similar cities, 50-60 per cent youth unemployment is frequent and incomes are only around half the national average. In parts of London, too, youth unemployment, especially amongst the coloured population, reaches 40 per cent and in cities such as the peripheral areas of Liverpool (in some neighbourhoods) even more. In the western suburbs of Sydney, Australia, unemployment among white youth, especially girls, is widespread and affects even some qualified young people.

2. Housing, environment and population mix

Housing and the attractiveness of the physical environment also play a considerable role in the decisions of the wealthier to leave certain urban areas although a few return to "gentrify" previously deprived areas in the larger cities. While many, who can, move to the suburbs, they leave behind many who cannot. The zones in which the latter live are "characterised by the age and poor quality of their housing" (Pflaumer, 1967). This is true in many OECD countries, in North America and Europe (Dickinson, 1967).

The extent of these problems varies from country to country. Much of the worst housing is located in the older city areas but by no means all. Blocks of flats built in the 50s and 60s in countries such as France or cities such as Manchester, are now in a state of advanced degradation. In some countries, the play of market forces interacting with particular pieces of legislation has led to the creation of areas of extremely poor housing and environment. In some, particularly, municipal policies have had the effect of concentrating "difficult" families in specific zones, sometimes in the city centre, as is frequently the case in North America, sometimes in more peripheral areas, notably in parts of Britain and France. In the latter especially, housing policies in conjunction with business development strategies have created zones of multiple deprivation on the edges of cities such as Paris. Among more serious social consequences of such re-location policies are the distancing of poorer populations from areas of employment, and encouraging a "ghetto" mentality, with its inherent juvenile delinquency and sense of isolation and alienation among their elders.

In many areas the net result of such trends and positions has been a decline in the richness of the urban population mix and a polarised distribution of population, creating, as Drewett points out, "a segregation of social and racial groups as the least mobile concentrate in particular urban zones. This is accentuated in Europe by the inflow of foreign guest workers" (1979, p. 24). With such populations comes the increased need for the provision of social services, income support measures and welfare centres.

This mix is especially important for more general consideration of social and fiscal policy. As a recent report by the U.S. Department of Housing and Urban Development pointed out, "trends in these characteristics reveal relative overabundance in central cities of citizens who are most likely to rely on public services and facilities coupled with a relative scarcity of income and tax capacity for financing such services and facilities" (HUD, Occasional Papers in Housing and Community Affairs, Volume 4, 1979).

There is, moreover, evidence that many local authorities in metropolitan zones are finding it increasingly difficult to meet their responsibilities in these areas. The decreasing tax base means that insufficient revenue is generated to provide the necessary services at a high level. The private sector is often equally deficient in filling the needs even of commercial services. Unable to flourish and grow in areas of low income, even shopping opportunities become reduced and inconvenient and frequently become high cost.

In summary here, as Haberer and Vonk writing of the Netherlands, Belgium, France, the United Kingdom and Germany say, "it is the increasing concentration of all kinds of minority groups (age, income, culture), added to the delapidating physical urban fabric, and the declining economic strength of the central cities that together are the building blocks for what is called the 'urban problem'" (1978, p. 18). In other words, pockets of especial deprivation have been created and these may have important and unwelcome social consequences beyond the boundaries of any specific areas. As Eversley (1972) observes: "Discontent will flow in the wake of the social pathology of the underprivileged community".

B. THE CONSEQUENCES FOR EDUCATION

Many aspects of the situation faced by the more disadvantaged quartiers of metropolitan zones have important repercussions on the type and quality of the education that is available. In many cases educational provision taken for granted elsewhere is absent and what is available is unused or underused because of a basic mismatch between offer and demand from local residents, whether children or adults. In many countries, such conditions also constitute constraints on the traditional goals and value systems sought by and inculcated by schools as described in (or implicit in) national educational policies. In areas of multiple disadvantage it is becoming increasingly evident that fundamental rethinking of the educational endeavour, from kindergarten through tertiary levels, is necessary.

The schools serving such areas are not spared the problems associated more generally with urban decline. In some cities, falling school rolls in inner-city areas may be seized as a chance to improve, perhaps dramatically, the staff-pupil ratio and to open up school buildings to community use. In most cases, however, social and economic problems have similarly severe repercussions on the education system. These educational difficulties concern the amount of "knowledge" that can effectively be transmitted to and absorbed by the pupils and students and are due to the physical, social and psychological conditions surrounding the education process. It is, of course, well known that these are the schools where discipline is hard to maintain and in the worst cases, where violence, both against teachers and between pupils is greatest. It is there that the children are most exposed to the dangers of different sorts of stress escape mechanisms (notably drugs) and where vandalism is an expensive epidemic.

These, however, are only the most apparent symptoms of the underlying problems. Other symptoms include large-scale truancy and even more widespread dropping out of school at the earliest possible opportunity after years of more or less passive attendance in formal schooling. Apathy, associated in many cases with withdrawal into a private self, is frequently at least as much a problem for educators. Indeed, in Australia, a recent study has found that some children are so passive in class that when questioned their teachers do not recognise their names and refuse to believe that such children are in fact members of their class. The general outcome, then, is wasted talents and the need for expensive supporting services, for (as said of the United States recently) urban poverty results at present in massive denial of educational opportunity and serious achievement losses for large numbers of inner-city students. Those who are not reached by special programmes are also educationally short-changed since the fiscal problems of urban areas have resulted in severely diminished offerings in areas such as art, music, athletics and special programmes for gifted and talented children.

The waste this represents is more than private tragedy. In very poor communities, the only resources on which local people can build are <u>human resources</u>. Lacking productive capital, local communities have to rely for their development on two sources: public aid (sometimes allied to private investment) and local community and individual skills and initiatives. Where these are under-developed and poorly organised, the only alternative is public aid.

At the same time, and in sharp contrast, as the discussion of urban policies during the Venice Conference showed, there is increasing need for public authorities and private innovators to be able to deal with a population better educated and more able to assess policy alternatives and to choose between opportunities when these occur. In times of often drastically curtailed funding, these choices need to become even more informed. Citizens' action and lobby groups are springing up in many OECD Member countries, and governments (as indicated by the French experience) are increasingly concerned to accommodate them. Decentralisation of funding procedures and even of the formulation of policy objectives and measures can only strengthen this movement.

There are, then, "negative" and "positive" reasons for taking a close look at the educational provisions at all levels within urban zones, particularly when the population is poor, mixed and subject to pressures in both housing and employment.

That education retains an important role in such areas is not in doubt. It has a very positive role to play in all aspects of development and improvement in the life chances of young people.

A draft statement prepared for the Council of Great City Schools in 1977 states the position forcefully:

"Urban schools and school systems ... should be placed in a central position in the formulation and development of any urban policy. It is more and more evident to urban school superintendents, board members, business and labour leaders that urban schools and school systems play an important role in stimulating economic recovery through employment and public works programmes. These institutions can play a significant role in reducing youth unemployment, especially that of urban minority youth; they can take on a greater role in reducing truancy, absenteeism and youth crime in our cities; they can play an instrumental role in reducing the number of welfare recipients; and most importantly, if provided with adequate funds and citizen support, they can and will improve the quality of education and student achievement in our cities, two factors which are critical to holding existing jobs and attracting businesses and investments back to the city. Various ... school districts have demonstrated their capability to get positive results in the identified areas, particularly when citizens perceive their schools as vital to the health and growth of their community." (M. Bins, C. Smith, "A National Urban Education Policy Statement" First Draft, December 1977.)

There are, moreover, particular reasons why schools can be seen as important in local economies, especially those that are multiply deprived. These are well expressed in the same document. Some refer specifically to the United States situation but many are more general.

"The demands of desegregation, the ban on discrimination against women, the high incidence of minority students, poor students, students with mental, physical and language handicaps and the need to retain recently hired minority professionals, make urban schools systems labor intensive. Because they are labor intensive they can provide many of the jobs needed to revitalise urban areas ... What is needed is not less but more specialists, instructional aides, support staff, tutors and qualified teachers. The special needs of inner-city schools also impose a necessity for continuous in-service training of teachers, administration, parents and support personnel. Guidance counsellors, school psychologists, psychometrists, dental hygienists and school nurses are also key factors in the success of any educational endeavor."

Job creation around these provides three pay-offs. It provides employment, helps prevent unemployment and helps people to help themselves and their children. The transformation of schools so as to make them into multi-purpose community centres multiplies these effects, notably in relation to employment. Without such an effort to improve job possibilities in poor areas, many countries are in danger of creating a permanent group of marginal workers whose lack of skills and early job experience will keep them chronically unemployed.

In terms of humanitarian and national social goals, too, changes need to be made to urban education systems. The goal of individual growth and subsequently, the finding of a satisfying job is getting harder to achieve nationally. In disadvantaged urban areas, helping young people to grow towards fulfilling their potential while nevertheless having realistic expectations about their post-school possibilities is an increasing and particularly difficult task.

One way to reconcile these two aims seems increasingly to lie in helping young people understand their communities and their problems and in helping them to grasp the different aspects of action necessary to improve them. In times of virtually no social and occupational mobility for poor urban populations through traditional employment channels, there seems much to be gained also for individuals and, indeed, their communities, by linking education more closely to local community development activities.

One further element in the situation should be mentioned here. Youth unemployment and, even more important perhaps, reduced possibility for skilled and supervisory or managerial employment, have an impact on education in even rather less disadvantaged areas. Difficulties of employment are widespread in cities, as elsewhere, and affect many "certified" as competent in particular skills by educational performance. Schools have traditionally organised their curricula (and the values and attitudes they impart) towards salaried employment in bureaucratically ordered organisations, whether public or private.

This assumption and the associated increased production of certificates of expertise in a narrow domain are now called into question. While the possession of a recognised diploma still helps many young people acquire a job and even a satisfying job, it can only help individuals in the competition. It cannot provide new jobs and the attitudes imparted are not those fundamental to the entrepreneurial qualities needed for new enterprise, whether in community service or private production. Although this is the "most educated" generation ever in most Member countries, many even "applied" credentials no longer have much power on the labour market. Le Monde, l'Année économique et sociale of January 1979 reported that in France it now takes almost five years for a generation of degree holders to find a permanent job. In 1977, young certificate holders of all kinds were "consistently finding lower-level jobs than their predecessors five years before".

In a few OECD countries, notably France, and Australia, and to some extent, the United Kingdom, girls are particularly hard hit. They are without a job longer and constitute a greater proportion of the unemployed, even when they hold technical and professional qualifications. This is particularly true in the service sector, the location of the traditionally "feminine" fields. In other countries, although nationally girls may be in a better position, there are pockets of severe female unemployment, especially in urban "ghettos" where commercial activity is much reduced. Education as a means to individual social mobility, as Jencks in the United States and Boudon in France among others have pointed out, was dependent on an expanding economic system and one providing ever-increasing numbers of high-level jobs. In recent years, not only have top jobs not been expanding but low-skilled jobs have been increasing, a situation likely to be exacerbated by the widespread use of micro-technology.

Schools, then, in such areas can no longer assume that greater production of diplomas is the answer to the unemployment problems of young people in many urban areas. It is no longer just a question of linking the supply of trained workers to the needs of local labour markets. Those markets themselves are too restricted; schools will have to rethink their "training" policies fundamentally.

C. URBAN POLICIES AND PRACTICES: THE NEED FOR A NEW APPROACH

1. Models and misdirections: the French urban planning experience

The Venice Conference was concerned to examine urban problems and policies insofar as they formed the background to, and environment of, educational issues and possible reforms. The first part of the meeting was therefore devoted to "setting the urban scene" as the prolegomena to the more detailed discussions of education and the site visits to innovations in the field in

Italy. M. Marc Durand-Viel, a senior member of the French public administration and in charge of government aid to local associations, used the occasion to indicate the changes in views of desirable urban policy as they have developed since 1945 and as they affect the educational issues of the present. What follows in sections a) and b) immediately below has been abstracted from his presentation. By taking France as an example, he indicates clearly the need for a significant shift in emphasis among urban planners if the problems outlined above are to be successfully addressed in the 1980s.

a) <u>Urban planning: principles and priorities</u>

In France, as elsewhere, urban planning in the 1950s and 1960s was highly directive. For over twenty years of triumphal urbanism, central authorities concentrated on controlling the development of big cities. Everything that seemed capable of helping with the task of forecasting, planning and bringing order to urban growth seen essentially in its spatial aspects was given precedence over the role (in urban development) of individuals and small groups. In these circumstances education could hardly be seen as anything other than just one among many services that a city must provide. A result rather than a means of urban development, the role of education was essentially to encourage labour mobility.

In that period, policies for the spatial development of cities aimed first at dealing with urgent housing needs. In the face of massive national population increase, an exodus of people from the countryside to the town at a rate of up to 200,000 persons a year and greater fertility among families, housing was primordial.

In its second phase, however, economic development considerations began to play an important role. The city became seen essentially as the "pole of economic development", and the more effective the greater the variety of services offered and the size of the local population.

To these concerns was added a particular kind of urbanistic ideology. Preference was given to the constitution of absolutely new ensembles, more and more planned where the central role was played by zoning and the aggregation of identical housing modules built around structuring axes. This kind of urbanism is more at ease with new cities, free from the constraints imposed <u>a priori</u> by existing inhabitants, towns that one builds first and fills only afterwards, towns produced by one man or one team and not by the mass of existing residents. This ideology can be seen translated into concrete in many French towns - Le Mirail in Toulouse, the <u>grands ensembles</u> of the suburbs, the early years of new towns between 1965 and 1970.

In other words, town planning became extremely centralising in revolt against the errors both of the "anarchic" building of the Paris suburbs early in the twentieth century and foreign models such as the extensive development characteristic of American cities. A whole arsenal of regulation and regulatory devices was introduced. With these went the growth of public and para-public agencies as the essential developers of city areas. "Together these resulted in areas without grace and built only with repeated forms."

In this model, education could only hold a limited place. Urban policies which aim at ever extending outwards the areas of a city and thus out beyond the confines of its existing residents leaves little room for active intervention by the education system in the creation of a humane and prosperous urban society. The official and direct role of education has been practically zero. Indeed, in France, information about urban phenomena, and a fortiori about the city where the school is situated, has never been included in any of the official curricula.

Education did, however, play an indirect role, which is not without importance for the present situation. It reinforced the cultural model which put the emphasis on modernity and change as superior social values. With the logic of both economic and urban development dominant in these years the real educative system was that which trains men for professional and geographical mobility and especially trains the young men as the future inhabitants of the new urban spaces being created.

Adoption of the central control views of urban planning also has more direct disastrous consequences. In France, the early necessity to deal with the most pressing urban problems, and notably housing, meant a concentration on quantity rather than quality. The result has been that, although city centres have often suffered adversely from outside development and the unequal distribution of financial resources, the degradation of the newest has been the most spectacular. Now, in the 1980s, the socially most disadvantaged are the newest areas, especially those with collective housing of a repetitive type, the towers and bars that characterise twenty or 80 ensembles in the Paris area and date from a maximum of 15 years ago. These are now totally degraded, especially on the sociological level and are the areas of greatest delinquency, lack of employment, lowest professional qualifications, least developed leisure activities, longest times of travel between home and work, and so on.

In short (and we continue to quote M. Durand-Viel), the major task of future years in France will be the remodelling of what has just been done rather than of the centres of cities which have lasted fairly well and been fairly well modernised by spontaneous mechanisms or public intervention.

b) From quantity to quality: a change in orientations, methods and objectives

There have, however, in recent years been alterations in all the elements of the equation. As M. Durand-Viel pointed out, in the wake of modifications in the economic structure and emphases in 1973-74, cities have been confronted with a different situation which has led to a re-orientation of urban policies and a modification of the role which might be played in them by education. Other factors in France have also altered. The acuity of the housing crisis has lessened and new demands for quality rather than quantity are being heard, both in respect to the environment and the housing itself. Finally, diverse technical and social factors have joined together to shake confidence in the ideology of growth, in the attraction of "modernity" erected as a principle for development and in the logical line previously established between the growth of the economy and the growth of great metropolitan centres.

These together have meant a new orientation for public policies. At the periphery large public housing projects have given way to private small-scale housing and small collective housing while in the inner city there is a new emphasis on renovation rather than demolition and considerable private initiative. Between the two, there has been a considerable effort to revitalise the suburbs through renovation and the provision of collective services, especially in education of all kinds.

At the same time, planning objectives have changed. There has been a shift of perspective such that the intention is no longer to push out the city boundaries but rather to reconquer the city's existing geographical and social space in a more qualitative development of the city itself. The planners are seeking to reshape the relations that already exist there such as the distances from home to work, individual and collective consumption of services and the balance between habitat, communication network and green space.

Finally, methods have changed too. While the share of public housing has decreased in general, changing housing trends have been encouraged by the switch to the provision of financial help to persons rather than to bricks and mortar. These facilitate the appropriations of space by a local inhabitant who is an owner rather than a tenant, who is permanent rather than transitory. In this way, the new provisions help to secure a proper base for local development initiatives. At the same time improvements are coming to depend more on the initiatives of individuals, small groups and enterprises, while the ability of political masters and technical experts to determine urban strategies seems to be diminishing. Although the progress of participation by the public in decisions about the orientation of urban policy is slow, it is getting more powerful and in the future may become decisive.

So there is a new attitude abroad in relation to both objectives and methods of urban planning on the part of both planners and planned. For this to be more than just demagogic or an expression of talent, the populations concerned need to learn much more about local environments and how to use the appropriate instruments of analysis. They also need to learn how to generate ideas amongst their neighbours and how to put propositions into action. They need education. They also need special programmes of help.

In line with these new orientations, methods and objectives, in France measures have been established and finance provided for disadvantaged urban areas. The areas concerned have been delineated by criteria such as unemployment and criminality rates, under-representation in education and local proportions of migrant workers. The programmes suggested were special because they were not imposed from above, appeal was not made to technicians to improve the area but an attempt was made to set up a viable system of communications between local authorities and local inhabitants. Problems arise because it is sometimes difficult to group local people into associations when such groupings do not already exist but the Ministry tries to determine a local programme in conjunction with the inhabitants.

Even more important here, attempts are being made at rehabilitation which is not restricted to the built environment. As M. Durand-Viel has said, it is relatively easy to perceive local demands when they are expressed in housing terms, e.g. when people want a house with a garden or a car park or to have the walls repainted. It is far harder to bring to the surface spontaneously elements of cultural demand, such as for communications network or for leisure facilities or for a new system of negotiation with a local developer. In these programmes, in order to encourage the formation of a strong local base the public authorities in France now agree to finance repairs to the built structures only if local organisations also present plans which are both educational and cultural. These are very diverse and range from an association for improving literacy to a group for organising the leisure of young people, linked to a group teaching them about the natural environment. In other words, the administrative condition for funding has now become the expression by local people of some collective wishes and plans. It is a far-reaching condition that has involved quite daring innovations.

These activities are effervescent, sometimes somewhat anarchic but the small resources that go into each make failures acceptable. Their success and their duration depend both on the dynamism of their creations and local public financial support. Much progress has been registered in this area over the last five years with the creation of specific funds in the different ministries concerned (culture, social action, quality of life) for innovatory activities. Work prepared for the first phase of the Eighth Plan suggests that between 1981 and 1985 these funds will become more widespread.

<u>A new role for education</u>. The common characteristic of all these programmes is the association of different partners that are involved (local users, residents, professionals, civil servants), the greater place recognised for education in the true sense and the improved possibilities for local inhabitants to make use of

their local city. The overall objective is to facilitate expression and communication within local areas. New jobs may eventually result from such renewed activity and self-confidence.

So far it has been suggested that the new orientations of urban policy make it possible for education to play a role. One may go further and say that active participation by education in local development is indispensable. General examples of this necessity may be given:

- the participation of users in decisions about their environment can only be successful in the long term if it is accompanied by a parallel progression in the information available to those concerned;

- rehabilitation of random social housing ensembles (known in France as "operations of habitat and social life") can only have a deep and long-term effect if, alongside the physical renovation efforts, educational programmes are also launched which seek to enrich the social fabric and the opportunities for local residents to emerge from their geographical and social isolation;

- a maximum return on socio-cultural facilities provided in disadvantaged areas (expensive both in investment and running costs) can only be attained by animation activities which encourage local residents to use them;

- the development of local employment, especially in new towns around Paris, pre-supposes the success of various educational activities touching all aspects of social life that it is hoped to develop there (financing, employment, collective services, consumption, culture and leisure).

Education, then, is seen at last as having a positive role to play in local development. These new orientations in France have made possible an evolution of the contribution of the education system to development since the changing city is that in which the school is embedded and is already known by each child. This familiarity facilitates the psychological appropriation of the urban environment. It is even possible to envisage a true apprenticeship by school children in the knowledge of their own urban environment. Such experiments were rare in the traditional school system, except on the initiatives of teachers in time outside the traditional subjects. They are more frequent in recurrent and vocational education and in those fields major links can now be established between the training institution and the local labour markets.

Outside the formal system of education, however, many new initiatives are being developed for local residents of all ages which seek to improve their knowledge and understanding of their city. Created by a variety of initiators, such as teachers, socio-cultural animateurs, non-traditional organisations, local residents associations, they seek many audiences and objectives and range from "universités de quartier" through cultural animation, centres for civic and social study and action and people's urban planning workshops to activities for young children such as "the Wednesday street" (there being no school in France on Wednesdays).

In summary we can say that we are beginning to see the emergence of new mentalities with a new respect for ideas emanating from local populations. These populations are saturated with the kind of development implied in "modernity" and too often associated simply with the provision of motorways, transport systems, grand equipment schemes and concrete everywhere. There is developing everywhere in Europe a cry for respect for persons. It is now much harder to bring into being projects such as new towns because the population wants to be consulted, to be able to criticise and if necessary to reject "progress", especially where it is brought in from outside.

Unfortunately, implementation of new initiatives is slowed because in France, as in many countries, the education system seems to find itself unable to respond in appropriate ways. Much of the education has to be done outside the formal school system, through the movements for popular education, through the little networks of people who constitute the universités de quartier. Even groups such as parent-teacher associations participate very little in these activities, especially in the most disadvantaged areas. While a beginning has been made, not enough has been done. It is time formal education took a more active role and facilitated the evolution of policy intentions into successful local development strategies.

2. Development with the people, by the people, for the people: Building up from below

a) Elements in rethinking: the strengthening of neighbourhood

The problems outlined above have, of course, been recognised now for a number of years even if, in many countries, their spread and intensity are only just being fully realised. A number of solutions are being put forward. Many of these, however, still depend on the linking of big ideas to big programmes; on the large-scale public financing (both of jobs and social services) and the administrative linking together of the big-spending social ministries with the frequently separate and low-funded planning authorities. At the beginning of the decade of the 1980s, neither of these seem likely to materialise. Many OECD Member governments are reducing public spending, notably in the social and educational spheres, in an effort to reduce inflation as a prerequisite to reducing unemployment. Co-operation between different public institutions recommended in so many reports, even in the school and community sphere, does not seem to be any nearer realisation.

In the face of the problems of urban deprivation, covering as these problems do poor housing, high rates of unemployment, low educational attainment, crime and social problems and yet others, it is coming to seem increasingly appropriate now to try small-scale local initiatives in many areas of life and in many urban zones. The problems of urban areas, while social and cultural in their manifestations, are frequently economic at heart. Their solution requires action on all fronts but first and foremost on the economic. This is not to say, however, that certain economic plans will work without prior changes in the neighbourhoods to which they apply. On the contrary, it is clear that in many areas self-help as well as publicly directed activities are necessary and these demand prior re-orientation of attitudes, expectations and above all of the images of self prevalent among youth and adults alike. This implies changes in attitudes and then of capabilities. It implies changes of orientation and a rethinking of many assumptions about what are seen as "natural" or "inevitable" trends and as the "right ways" of approaching problems and doing things whether they be developmental or educational.

Thus, in the face of increasing disadvantage and inequalities of life chances, of rising private costs and decreasing public resources, the necessity arises to rethink fundamentally a number of policy approaches. In the view of many, such rethinking should be based on the following principles:

- increased public participation in the decisions that affect both their family members' lives and their environment;

- increased self-help activities in the provision of necessary social services, whether they be creches, old people's services or others;

- increases in self-help improvement of the built environment and of housing;

- a change of attitude such that people become aware of the possibilities of their area and of their possible role in improving it;

- a re-orientation at the same time in relation to economic activity and to social facilities so that self-help in employment (by communities and individuals) also becomes a possibility;

- a more flexible and imaginative approach on the part of public policy-makers and the controllers of public finances and notably a "facilitating" rather than a directive attitude by public authorities; the provision of tools for self-help and access to outside assistance where necessary;

- an increase in both "technical" and "personal" or "attitudinal" skills among local populations;

- a reconsideration of priorities in the allocation of public funds.

Devising policies for the economic, social and cultural revival of deprived city areas involves consideration of a variety of strategies. Reviewing the situation in Member countries, an OECD planning group recently suggested that the following should be examined:

- attraction strategies which would increase job availability in areas currently experiencing employment decline through attracting firms to locate or relocate in these cities;

- generation strategies to increase employment through the generation of new firms either by local entrepreneurs or by attracting external capital;

- stabilisation strategies to arrest decline and retain existing employment;

- community development strategies to create new employment through improving the community's housing stock, amenities and the like.

In the development of these new approaches one of the key elements will be the strengthening of the neighbourhood and the possibilities of action by residents of small local areas. A report by the OECD Policy Project Group on urban decline underlined the importance of the neighbourhood, for some aspects of urban decline do not lend themselves to policy prescription at an aggregate level. The primary importance of the neighbourhood is that it is the setting in which people live and from which they derive their overall sense of well-being. It is, in short, the area with which they identify most readily and in which it is probably easiest to organise action groups. The neighbourhoods are the "building blocks of the city"; strategies to strengthen them are strategies for strengthening the city.

Doing this requires educational policies that relate to the real problems faced by the neighbourhoods concerned. Not only must the curriculum "fit" the situation of the community, but if the training offered is to reach the right members of the group and be assimilated by them, it must, to some extent, spring from their felt needs. They must feel that they both benefit from it and to some extent control it. A willingness on the part of staff, pupils and parents alike to find issues and seek new ways of presenting them is primordial. New information has to be generated and passed on. Changes need to be made at all levels of the educational tree. Examples given in the cases presented below illustrate a number of possibilities and indicate promising practices in diverse Member countries. The importance of these innovations is recognised, however, by all, even though degrees and methods of implementation may vary. In other words, it seems to be generally accepted that:

"   as new information is assimilated by a community; as an improved understanding of its problems, needs and aspiration is acquired; as it learns to make common decisions, thoughtfully, fairly and deliberately; as these things happen within a community, it indeed "develops". Yet to ensure such development, such favourable growth, is no simple matter; only through "community education" can it be achieved" (in "Education for Community Development", an unsigned article in the Community and Junior College Journal, Washington D.C., March 1980, p. 4).

Such education necessitates a change away from the national goals implicit in "up and out" educational policies which deliberately encourage individual social mobility through professional upward movement, usually involving geographical relocation. Such policies take individual, gifted children and give them the tools (diplomas, know-how) to move elsewhere and to transform their social and psychological identity. Community development requires a different orientation; taking it seriously means giving members of the community confidence to stay and act in their own neighbourhood, confidence that they can improve local conditions and, perhaps above all, the will to link their own destinies to that of their area.

b) The bases for new policies: education and economic regeneration

Many of the arguments in favour of such new policies hinge on allowing a greater role for local initiatives of all kinds. It would seem from what has gone before that this approach should have two points of attack. The first concerns the revitalisation of the economic base. The second, the re-orientation of attitudes. In practice, they may be expected to go together, and both the formal education system and non-formal training schemes have specific contributions to make.

A healthy local economy, as a recent report has emphasized, is "essential to the wider well-being of the community. A range of jobs available within easy travelling distance is essential to prosperity, self-respect and harmonious living". To achieve such a result it is impossible, especially in the straitened economic circumstances of the decade of the 1980s, for public money and job creation programmes to act alone (Urbed, 1978). "Third sector" activity, part public, part private, is being proposed in Europe as a solution (Delors, 1978). In both Europe and the United States the emphasis is on the "public-private" partnership, on acting at the public-private interface in various ways. Increasingly, Member countries are trying new routes, new tactics, using public money to leverage private funds as "seed" money for innovative strategies of many kinds.

Efforts to link public and private interests and resources in economic activity and "new look" revitalisation plans for deprived metropolitan areas, whether old or newly created, frequently contain the following major policy elements.

First, there is a recognition on the part of urban policy-makers that a fresh look should be taken at the economic base in major cities. They suggest that, while the closure of a major employer is dramatic in these areas, the greater part of employment is provided in small businesses, of fewer than 200 employees and frequently much smaller, fewer than 50 or even 20. In the inner London borough of Islington, for example, 85 per cent of local firms employ less than 20 people (Arclight, July 1979, p. 3). In Manchester small manufacturing firms provide 85 per cent of employment. In the United States, a report by Birch at MIT in 1978 suggested that large proportions of new jobs were created by small and medium companies (HUD Economic Development. New Roles for City Government, 1979, p. 45).

Second, policy action and emphases are increasingly being oriented towards entrepreneurs. These may be private enterprise activities or they may be community based. In this sense, the word entrepreneur refers to an individual who is creating an activity that is either wealth-creating or service-producing where neither existed before or where existing ones need developing. These entrepreneurs may use private or public funds, or, increasingly, both, to create activities which involve employment for themselves and usually others. The "enterprises" they create may take the form of traditional micro-businesses, working for the profit of the owner, or of co-operatives, of "workshops" which may or may not make profits. They may be community-based organisations that aim to make a profit but to plough the profits back into the provision of community services or the creation of further enterprises. The best known examples of these are found in the United States, where they take the form of Community Development Corporations (CDCs) or similar organisations.

These efforts are based on the idea that every bad condition in poor areas reinforces other bad conditions and that as poor economic and social environments weaken individual attempts to react, a broad community effort is necessary. The strategy of community economic development is "essentially a plan of action to build new resources that will strengthen the community internally and in its relations with the outside world. It begins with a co-ordinating, planning and action tool like a CDC, to carry out this action" (Community Development Corporations, CCED, 1975, p. 2). Such "entrepreneurial" organisations with a community base are an important element in new urban neighbourhood revitalisation strategies.

No less important in some places are community "self-help" activities linked to youth employment schemes. Certain of these schemes aim specifically to improve the housing available and other parts of the immediate built environment. In Italy, in Venice, such schemes operate under Law Nº. 285 for youth employment to help restore the historic town centre. In the United States, housing rehabilitation through local youth schemes using federal and other public funds is becoming increasingly common and provides on-the-job training for many local unemployed youth, frequently high school drop-outs. In conjunction with "sweat-equity" urban homesteading, these schemes may be the start of wider development-activities. In East Harlem, for instance, local groups of ex-drug addicts, often ex-prison detainees, have not only turned to housing rehabilitation but also presented schemes for new local commercial and service activities. They recognise that housing is not sufficient; people need to have jobs and access to services as well.

Such activities, while they may seem largely symbolic in the face of the massive scale of the problems faced by many deprived urban communities, have extremely important demonstration effects. They indicate that improvement is possible; that local people have skills that are valuable, both to the individual concerned and to their families and communities. Those that are aimed at youth have one further element of fundamental importance; they provide a real job and clearly useful work for the youngsters concerned. They are not "make work" activities.

Education can contribute to the success of these new policies in a number of ways. First, in urban areas, schools and colleges are major centres of expertise and skilled personnel. These can be of immediate benefit in development activities. They can help new and existing entrepreneurs, both individual and "community" ones. They can help train young people to become sensitive to their local environment and create both the wish and the skills to improve it. They can help young people see the role they can play in the social services of the area, both formally organised and those which involve "youth as resources for youth", in settling their own problems. They provide technical skills.

In this and in other ways, schools can help provide the pre-conditions for development. They help to instill more confident attitudes into young people. They can contribute to creating a deep sense of the community's own identity and its needs. This can be done through the teaching-learning process itself, and notably through much greater use of action or experiential learning techniques. It can also be done through the provision of culural and leisure activities which form a meeting place and a basis for the cohesion necessary to make community-based activities work.

Schools and colleges, therefore, have a dual role to play in urban development policies. First, they constitute resources to be used by the community and ways need to be found whereby specific development policies can use these resources to the full. Second, they can take an active role in preparing the local community, especially young people, to grasp the development opportunities that are available and to create new ones.

In summary of this section, then, we can say that many major cities in OECD countries are in crisis. Long-term social and economic forces have created a situation in which pockets of disadvantage have persisted and even become worse. Such disadvantages include poor housing, inadequate social services, scarce employment opportunities, poor leisure facilities and frequently an inadequate and inappropriate education system. Planning policies and much educational endeavour, while trying to achieve other important goals, have even exacerbated the situation in many poor areas.

There is, however, a new recognition among policy-makers that local development, using local initiatives, people, expertise and resources to a maximum, may be the only way forward. Given this new policy focus, a series of new approaches would seem to be necessary. The solution of the problems requires the adoption of flexible, often small-scale responses. Not only must many outside public resources continue to be devoted to helping disadvantaged areas, but education in all its forms must take a more active role and be used more systematically to assist with the creation of new opportunities, economic, social and cultural. It must help all concerned, of all ages, to use to a maximum their own and their communities' resources, so many of which are at present sadly under-utilised.

Taking this role seriously involves educators and educational institutions of all kinds in being prepared to experiment, adopt new attitudes, to develop new curricula and teaching methods, to work towards new aims and ideals without, however, losing sight of the best of the existing ones. (We must here stress that much of the best education available in Member countries is provided in major cities. Urban education in general is of high quality and uses a multitude of extra outside resources. The problems occur in pockets within the conurbations considered.)

Successes in this field are already widespread in many OECD countries. The following sections present some important innovatory practices and strategies as examples of these new approaches.

Part Two

EDUCATION AND THE PRE-CONDITIONS FOR DEVELOPMENT

A. ATTITUDES, VALUES, INTERESTS

School experiences in poor urban areas have particular importance for the lives of the students concerned, not least because of family influences on their development; these are likely to be for the worse rather than the better. Resigned or depressed parents, frequently "on welfare", inadequate surroundings and alienated peers all constitute weighty factors creating a similar set of attitudes in the younger generations.

In these areas, too, young people are often exposed to stresses and tensions, to physical and "moral" dangers which are largely unknown to their rural and even to their more advantaged urban and suburban counterparts. They face especially great difficulties in seeing the "relevance" of school, in submitting to the discipline of passive learning and in dealing with the anonymity of large schools. Largely failing within the academic or even vocational streams, they lack self-confidence and seek to establish themselves in activities which attribute no value to formalised learning. This "counter culture" of disadvantaged youth has its roots, therefore, in the school as well as the community and as the community gets into a downward spiral of decay or expands so fast that it becomes disorganised, so its young people easily start on the path that leads to socially unacceptable behaviour and an extremely narrow range of subsequent life possibilities.

Many experts feel that much formal schooling in such areas does not take sufficient account of the essentially low opinion the young people there hold of themselves and the confusion of values to which they are subject. At the same time, many students have too few occasions to participate in socially meaningful activities. Many young people are "placed in the charge of institutions that insulate them from society's mainstream, condemned to uselessness at a critical moment in their development ... [and] cannot be expected to prepare for the complexities of adult life without participating in significant activities ...Young people are starving for lack of maturity-producing experiences" (National Commission on Resources for Youth, Report to HEW, Office of Youth Development, Youth Participation, 1975). This report suggests that youths need to be involved in responsible, challenging actions that meet genuine needs, with opportunity for planning and/or decision-making affecting others, in an activity whose impact or consequences extend to people other than the youth participants themselves.

Taking this finding seriously has important consequences for the organisation of teaching and the choice of curricula appropriate for schools in deprived urban areas, and indeed possibly for other schools too. It involves fundamental rethinking of the aims and methods of educational practice from primary school through to tertiary and adult further education.

As a first step in this re-organisation it is necessary to recognise that the traditional goals of education, most strongly inculcated in the "academic" streams but implicit in a watered-down form in most secondary studies, will need re-examination. It may be necessary to reassess the widespread assumption that young people are essentially the passive recipients of other people's knowledge, a passivity only leavened by the occasional piece of group project work. They will increasingly need to be considered, not only as individuals with particular learning needs and capacities, but also as members of the local community, likely to remain within it and operate within a specific socio-economic and cultural structure. That in turn may further involve re-orienting learning so that the skills needed for understanding, coping with and ultimately modifying in positive ways that environment hold an important place in the curriculum.

It seems to be widely agreed that this is necessary for the sake of the development of the potential of young people themselves, even without considering the effects of new methods in the creation and implementation of social development policies. It also seems, however, that the two may be satisfactorily linked. To this end, action-learning and youth participation in a wide range of activities that affect both their own education and that of others as well as being useful to the community need greater emphasis. Used on occasion in many Member countries, such methods are frequently reserved for the least academic. All young people could benefit.

Students in many levels of education can take part in a wide range of such activities. They may cover:

- curriculum building (varying from social studies to public health);

- youth as teachers (tutoring younger children, bilingual education, etc.);

- youth as community manpower (in-school, credit-carrying activities);

- youth as entrepreneurs (we return to this below).

Other activities are related to social service activities outside the school, although sometimes organised with the help of school personnel. These include:

- youth as community problem-solvers;

- youth as communicators;

- youth as resources for youth.

There are thus specific attitudes and skills that a school may help to inculcate and for which young people have little preparation elsewhere. Some involve service to others and to the community. Some involve self-confidence and ability to take decisions in concert with peers, whether at school, at work, or in community organisations.

Such new skills and attitudes may well be needed, for example, in new employment situations. The encouragement of enterprises in urban development requires not only technical assistance in their birth and growth but also the possibility to recruit young people with appropriate sets of attitudes as well as special professional skills. Both the latter may require conscious inculcation in the milieux concerned. In economic development plans, work organisations, whether wholly public, community or public-private funded, are frequently of a type that aims to involve all the members of the enterprise in decision-making. Workshops, co-operatives, community-development corporations, school-based enterprises demand not only initiative on the part of their members but a willingness to work together rather than individually or for the immediate pecuniary benefit of members. This willingness, this ability to act co-operatively, is vital to the functioning of a productive organisation that operates with few formal rules, where each member's productivity counts towards the success of the enterprise and where decisions need to be taken about reinvestment for expansion into much-needed community services, for example. (See a number of examples in "Et chacun créait son emploi", in Autrement, September 1979). Young people from deprived backgrounds are frequently refused work by outside employers because they are perceived as unreliable, poor time-keepers, careless and generally unco-operative. While these reactions are frequently exaggerated, they are often a real problem to traditional firms and to "alternative" work and leisure organisations. Such attitudes carry over into community activities, too. Schools can and in some places do make deliberate efforts to overcome these and to help here.

1. Learning the locality: local studies and environmental education

a) The contribution of secondary schools

A major pre-condition for effecting changes in the local community is increasing knowledge of it among its inhabitants. The knowledge can take many forms; some involve greater awareness of the geographical layout of the area and the relationship the locality bears to others and notably the major economic centres closest to it. This is important to the "psychological appropriation of the urban space" referred to above in relation to France.

But two other kinds of local knowledge are particularly crucial. The first concerns understanding the nature of and processes behind the social and economic structure of the area, both past and present. Within this sphere comes information about housing stock, the employment structure, the population mix, and how each developed to be what can be experienced daily by local residents.

The second involves knowledge about the operations of the major agencies functioning in the community. Most of these will be public, including local councils, welfare agencies, health facilities. Others may be voluntary associations. Others will be private or para-public, such as the many agencies mediating between public funding and private projects, agencies widespread in the United States and developing elsewhere.

Gaining all these kinds of knowledge and understanding forms the basis for a "community audit" on which action can be planned in a coherent manner. "Learning the locality" is fundamental to an assessment of local resources, physical, economic and human, as well as to pinpointing accurately both the major loci of problems and possible solutions.

The education system has an important role to play in this, both in in-school courses for primary and secondary level children and in classes for adults. The curriculum offered needs to include important sections of local studies, in history, in geography, in social studies and even in technical studies or science. It needs in the widest as well as the narrowest sense to include important components of environmental education.

In many countries, those responsible for curriculum development are beginning to become aware of the degree to which present courses exclude local and environmental issues. In secondary schools in many Member countries the curriculum is generally divided into science and humanities. In the words of one recent British urban research report, this division "leaves out a third vital area, that of subjects concerned with making and doing".

Such lacuna have a number of consequences. They mean, for example, that academically-oriented children often have no contact with art subjects, although they may well be destined for careers in which they would make crucial decisions about the built environment (Department of the Environment, 1978b). They also mean that other children are unable to make the links between what they learn at school and what they see and experience in their communities.

Environmental education does not have to become "yet another" course in its own right. On the contrary, the report concludes that it must be both theoretical and experiential and incorporated into traditional subject areas. It should be concerned with allowing children to become sensitive to their environment and to understand the reasons for its deficiencies as the first step to improving it. It should seek principally to teach understanding of relationships between social, economic and aesthetic considerations and their consequences for the built form. The emphasis should be on local studies, with locally produced materials, bringing educational and environmental interests together. The authors of the report recommend that "the initial emphasis needs to be on inner-city partnership areas" and that the relevant government departments "should urgently explore ways of introducing an environmental education element into the Urban Programme and, in particular into the inner-city partnership schemes" (idem).

The same report also recommends educational programmes outside the schools, to be in the form of a network of Urban Studies Centres to constitute resources available to adults and children alike.

Initiatives have been taken along lines similar to those suggested in the British report in a number of OECD countries. In Britain itself, for example, an 'O' level examination paper in "architectural awareness" was introduced by one of the main examining boards in 1980. The syllabus will include historical study of styles of architecture but also the "effects of the industrial revolution on workers' homes and how to lay out a water supply for a new house" (from a report in Building Design, 16.3.1979, p. 5). Urban Studies Centres will support such initiatives by running complementary classes for adults, as does the one at Canterbury in England on local industry, planning and alternative technology.

In England and Wales, the Schools Council has been active in developing geography-based courses that teach about and involve children in the analysis of their local environment. One scheme, intended for the 14-16-year-old age group has been particularly successful and has now been adopted by a wide variety of schools and used for a wide range of children. Working in close co-operation with Local Education Authorities, the scheme has led to the establishment of a network of local curriculum groups of teachers producing materials for local studies. These groups are co-ordinated by regional organisers, themselves under a Project Director. By 1978 virtually all LEAs in England and Wales (102 out of 104) were in the scheme and 40 per cent of schools with 14-16-year-old pupils used at least some of the material generated in their curricula. A similar project is now being developed for 16-19-year-olds.

The Schools Council has also recently set up a project on the Art and the Built Environment for 16-19-year-olds which is being tried in a dozen or so institutions with the aim of finding ways to extend students' perceptions and feelings for the built environment and their capacity for visual appraisal and discrimination. This scheme developed out of a project undertaken in Pimlico, a mixed inner-city area of London, involving collaboration between a school and a team of local architects who participated both in planning and in teaching. Architects have also been involved elsewhere. The Royal Institute of British Architects (RIBA) collaborated with Newcastle University in 1977 in creating the Newcastle Workshop. Financed by Job Creation Scheme funds, the centre brings together planners, teachers, advisers, architects, children and community groups. A Schools Advisory Group has been testing the projects and school children have been using the resources of the workshop.

In Italy there is much concern about the future of the central areas of the country's many historic cities. In a country with so many magnificent buildings in need of restoration and with many areas in need of economic regeneration, it is especially important that local inhabitants be involved in the process of renovation. City educational authorities have begun to develop a number of innovatory programmes aimed at sensitising children to their heritage and involving them in its preservation. The first step is to teach them about what is there. To this end, children need to be taken around the urban area and taught to look at it with new eyes. In Venice, for example, the Assessorato alla Pubblica Istruzione has developed a series of "journeys" around Venice undertaken by primary school children. Known as Itinerari Educativi, these journeys cover each time different aspects of the past and present life of the city and introduce children to the economic structure of the present and the dominant local activities.

One concerns, for instance, local artisanal activities. Working through the professions linked to buildings it moves through those producing beautiful objects in household use and on to those currently offering personal services. The place of each is explained and in the illustrated books that go with the journeys the child is invited to look out for specific things on his or her visits around the local area and, while engaging in daily activities, to analyse their organisation (hairdressers, builders, etc.). The teacher's guide is drawn up so as to indicate the principal analytical categories to be used. Some concern the economic structure more generally, such as the organisation of the factors of production, the relationship between men and machines, the scientific organisation of work, legal aspects, especially relating to artisan activities, the historical aspect of the division of labour. Others then relate more specifically to the place of artisan production - concern economic organisation and the organisation of artisan activities, the division of work between master and journeymen or apprentices in each enterprises. The technology and techniques used and the reasons for the decline in artisan production (links to the industrial revolution, etc.) are also explained.

Some of the most outstandingly successful examples of curriculum design in local studies at school level come from the United States. One example in particular is worth quoting here, even though it was developed in a town smaller than the cities of the present report for there is no reason why it should not be repeated elsewhere. Enfield, an old mill town on the Connecticut River, has a high school which has a social studies programme that typifies what may be done by secondary school students creating their environmental education curriculum themselves. Started by a student of 16 years, it soon won the support not only of the school's authorities but of outside bodies, including companies who helped with materials and equipment. The desire for 'relevance' encourages the asking of locally-oriented questions - What does an expressway do to a community? How can we save our landmarks? What happens to an immigrant if he comes here to live?

The Social Studies Laboratory at Enfield soon spawned a Living History Unit which made sound slide projects on subjects related to both the physical and built environment and to the social and economic structure and the values and relationships generated in the local community. One film, for instance, documented the relationships between the local police, the community and young people. Another thing they did was to go out into other schools with the "Lab Charts" they designed themselves as a multi-media teaching device on given themes. The project has enabled students to produce information as well as learn about their local community and has encouraged many students to work on areas of relevance to local questions.

The Lab has proved its worth also as a pedagogical device, even with the less academic students. Participation in its operations has a lasting effect on the learner and on his perception of what he or she can do. It has led to a more mature and more useful understanding of the essential elements of the learning process. Students begin to see staff as fellow researchers after knowledge and to appreciate that knowledge is not in "pat" answers. As they begin to understand these things, a recent report on the project stated, students grow in self-confidence and self-motivation. Success is due to the fact that each contribution is retained and becomes a resource for other students, teachers and the people of the town. Something concrete has emerged from student work. (Information derived from Chapter 2 of New Rules for Youth in the School and the Community, National Commission on Resources for Youth, 1974.)

In France, too, there has been a recent move to develop a curriculum that permits an important place to be allocated to the study of local history and local and economic and social structures. The Centre National de la Documentation Pédagogique has launched a call for the development of curriculum materials on the theme of the France of the Future. This call has been taken up by several of the Centre's local constituent bodies who have prepared audio-visual and written materials on different aspects of French life. Realising that the France of the future cannot be predicted without a better knowledge of the past and present and particularly the past and present of local areas, much effort has been devoted to improving students' understanding of the major themes affecting their existence as members of particular regions and particular cities. The Curriculum Development Centre of the Lille area, a highly industrialised and long urbanised zone, has been particularly active in the field. Multi-media curriculum materials have been created by the Centre in line with the collaboration of local television teams, with staff in local teacher-training colleges and with local families and people involved in activities concerning the themes chosen.

One set of materials treats the question of immigration in the region. A film made by local people presents interviews with immigrants from North Africa living and working in Lille and shows their problems, disabilities and aspirations. Towards the end, the film shows a forum organised in a local primary school in which the children question a group of immigrant women. Accompanying documents both complete the analysis of the situation and indicate to the teacher useful ways to integrate the materials into a variety of courses, including the teaching of the French language.

Other films and multi-media materials are specifically concerned with the local economic situation, both past and present. In each the approach is similar, to emphasize the local, using documents from local archives, interviews with citizens using the oral history method, interviews with employers, with workers, with the unemployed, with families long established or new to the area. Some discuss the industrial revolution and its long-term consequences for the area; others present the life of specific local industries, such as the coalmines; yet others seek more generally to deepen students' knowledge about various urban centres in their areas and the employment that might be open to them as local workers.

In Britain a rather different approach has sometimes been tried. Several schools have introduced courses which involve students in surveys in their local areas and in participation in local community facility improvement schemes as part of their general education. In Lambeth, a disadvantaged suburb of inner London, for instance, this has been tried in several schools, from primary through secondary to upper-secondary.

In one school, for example, sixth form students took part in a series of housing survey projects with the assistance of the housing group "Shelter". These schemes seem to show clear positive results. After the Shelter project was over, teachers reported increased community interest and involvement by the participants with a number of students helping outside school hours with children's playgrounds, toy-mending, etc. on a voluntary basis.

Through a similar project undertaken with a much younger age-group in the same borough, the children acquired greater self-confidence and a feeling that they could in fact improve their surroundings. Even projects that "fail" in themselves may turn out to have positive returns for their participants who acquire useful information and action skills. These are particularly important to poor populations who, perhaps more even than their more fortunate co-citizens, must frequently deal with official agencies of all kinds and insist on their rights in relation to welfare and other schemes. The extent of misunderstanding of their situation is sometimes hard to over-estimate, as one of the Lambeth projects showed. In that area, even after a not very successful project, one youngster of "secondary" age was led to exclaim that he had discovered that he could write a letter to the Council without being sent to prison (Inner London Study, Lambeth, Schools, 1978, p. 7). Schools must, therefore, both provide information and build the self-confidence needed to use it.

b) Tertiary level initiatives

"Learning the locality" continues to be important beyond the level of the secondary school. Institutions of further and higher education should be involved in the task and may be instrumental in providing learning experiences that form the basis for further activities such as the "community audit".

American Community Colleges often play a particularly important role in this connection. Indeed, in the eyes of many, the colleges' most frequent mission is to provide an educational environment particularly propitious to the realisation of individual potential through the encouragement of locally-oriented initiatives and courses geared to local needs. (Examples will be given in a later section of such initiatives in the purely economic sphere.) The approach is in many ways essentially that of one taking the individual as a member of his local as well as his national community. Some of the colleges attempt to provide courses specifically concerned to awaken the individual to his or her environment and to provide both knowledge and encouragement to analyse the individual's relationship and responsibilities to family, community and society, "to cultivate values and skills in critical thinking, decision-making and problem-solving approaches to personal and societal dilemmas", to awaken students "to an understanding of their historical and cultural heritage".

In addition, colleges such as the Florida Junior College at Jacksonville, aim particularly to promote education for both "individual and community" and to develop "a comprehensive curriculum to address the diverse needs of the individual and the community". By learning specific personal skills students are expected both to learn about and to increase their potential for acting in their local community.

In Jacksonville, too, the Office of Curriculum Services of the Community Colleges collaborated with the State Department of Education in the production of a list of priorities in educational provision to be presented to the local authorities. Using local resources such as surveys and daily editions of the local newspapers, a list of priorities and changes in priorities is regularly drawn up. Priorities are determined by their number of occurrences in individual surveys and local newspapers over the preceding year. Such programmes can potentially form part of the basis for a community audit; in this way, even though it has limitations of an obvious kind, information is gathered on a community's expressed priorities. A similar method could also be used to establish a list of community resources.

In other countries, teaching about the locality is also done in part by adult education centres which can be used as well as other members of the community. In Britain, for instance, a network of Urban Studies Centres has been built up and is being expanded. These serve a number of objectives. One of their central functions is to provide a specialist learning base for schools, and resource centre for teachers. But, as Hall and his colleages report, they can also provide adult courses for professionals and councillors, a meeting place for local groups, and a point through which the local planning authority and other organisations can distribute environmental information. They are a quick and economical way of producing teaching material apposite to local needs and topical (<u>op. cit.</u>).

If Urban Studies Centres provide a meeting place for school children and adult members of the community and local authority representatives, schools themselves can also provide a focal point for different groups concerned with the improvement of the local environment. Here again an example may be taken from Britain where it has been said that one of the most important new moves in developing the skills of decision-making and participation has been the movement of some city planning departments in education. This interaction occurs in a variety of ways; the planners not only provide raw data but also advise and help teachers, produce classroom material and visit schools explaining current issues and evaluating work. A number of other bodies also participate. Among these are the Town and Country Planning Association Education Unit, Heritage Education and the Council for Urban Studies Centres. Some local councils such as Hammersmith in London have appointed a full-time education officer specifically to liaise with schools and colleges and to find out the kinds of resource material they need. Others have set up special environmental education working parties to bring planning and education departments together so as to encourage the best use of local resources.

Finally here one should consider the elements of the training of the professionals themselves who are going to be most closely concerned with the shape of the environment in their working lives. These include architects, planners, surveyors, engineers and others such as health officials, as well, of course, as school teachers themselves.

2. <u>Territorial education: an Italian experiment</u>

Linking education more closely with development may in some cases involve fundamental rethinking of the aims of the educational process. This may be particularly the case in adult education and/or where the secondary school curriculum has included no elements of local life or culture. It may also be the case in a country where the curriculum has always been centrally controlled and determined. Much of what happens in education "on the ground" is also a function of the research that is done in education, of the organisation of the discipline into separate blocks of knowledge at university level and in teacher-training colleges. Such a division, as taught in educational institutions, tends to cause the break up of the unity of knowledge as experienced by pupils, whether of school age or adult.

Many schools in many different countries are trying to come to grips with this problem. Experiments of the kind already described are often attempts to overcome such fragmentation by relating the teaching-learning experience in schools to "real-life" situations outside the classroom. Some experiments have gone even further and taken the local community, defined as the intermediary group between the family and the nation, as the basis for developing a curriculum of immediate relevance to adult learners in the area.

Our next example, described in some detail so that it may provide a model, is a particularly successful experiment linking education to local development undertaken by a team of researchers at the University of Naples. It indicates, as few others do, a down-to-earth approach in a community that is unused to systematic self-analysis and to self-generated improvement schemes. The research started from the viewpoint that:

"those who theorise the 'death of education', despite all their extremism, have highlighted a real problem in education by denouncing loud and clear the <u>state of separation which exists between education which derives from everyday experience</u> - which has the greatest effect on the real formation of man - and <u>education which is imparted within institutions</u> which should exercise a crucial function with respect to the former."
(P. Orefice, 1978, p. 1 of the English text. Emphasis in the original.)

The question, in Orefice's view, is how to relate more closely "formal education" and "informal education" because only in that way can "institutionalised education avoid being alienated from real life and spontaneous education develop its creative potential".

The project, known as MOTER, was started in 1978 and concerned four small communities in close proximity to the city of Naples. (Again, MOTER developed in smaller urban centres but could be transposed to city neighbourhoods; it was in fact a previous experience in Neapolitan suburbs that led to the idea.) The project, funded by the Education Office of the Regional Authority of Campania, sought to link formal and non-formal education by concentrating on the educational demands emerging from the local community in a given area. It has as its context the devolution to the new regional authorities of development powers previously held by the national government. Under the new system, participation in decisions about education and many other aspects of local life (through the Local Health Unit, the <u>Comprensorio dei Communi</u>, etc.) is thus explicitly sought.

It became clear, however, that such participation might well be problematic in some communities and that the basis on which it might be improved in quantity and quality was education. But that education had to be related to local needs. Local inhabitants had to be enabled to analyse the elements of the situation in a systematic and coherent way they had not previously experienced. Project MOTER was an attempt to bring this about.

The project began with a background enquiry, a "dynamic photograph", to bring to light aspects of the social, economic, educational and administrative structure that could be used in shaping the programme, the aim of which was to develop participation by local groups in research and through that to pinpoint problematic themes and priorities in the development of local life. Political parties, trade unions, farmers' groups, the local radio all took part as well as schools of all levels and adult education programme organisers. Meetings held with such bodies suggested the themes for the detailed research - family and the structure of maritime employment; the crisis of local culture; the problems of the local cultural heritage in relation to economic development; agriculture; health, and so on. The contacts made in the course of collecting the necessary data themselves gave the research procedure an educative quality since the local people had to make individual efforts to clarify the various aspects of local life.

During the research it became evident that many groups had difficulty expressing themselves; it was not easy, for example, to translate the analytical terms used by the researchers into the language of such groups as the local fishermen. For people with little schooling and adults far removed from study or from political and trade union militancy, "participation was concentrated once more on giving vent to feelings rather than on the meaning or direction of the talk" and new methods had to be developed to cope with this (P. Orefice, 1979, pp. 22-23).

The result at this stage was a series of "forms" used as a basis for discussions in meetings of the local organisations. Each form used cartoon-type images of people and places, linked together by a series of arrows and questions to invite local people to analyse systematically a given question, to help them to begin to perceive linkages between different elements and to seek answers to the questions indicated, many of which had been previously unperceived. The form on economic, political and social life had, for instance, a page on the situation in local education. Two pictures showed the numbers of children in lower secondary school and the numbers in upper-secondary school. Side by side the great drop in numbers between the two cycles stood out clearly and the readers were invited to answer the question of where the others had gone and so on. The analysis thus made formed the basis for discussions in schools and in open public meetings, and ensured continuity of approach.

The next stage was to programme the more formally defined activities of permanent education. Here wall-charts on such subjects as the municipal area, productive activities, trade unions and public administration, school and health and cultural behaviour, enabled local people to have a "reflected image" in which they could recognise themselves. Local radio also contributed by special programmes and school children produced visual presentation materials. The sometimes heated discussions generated contributed to the self-education process and to bringing to light people's most urgent needs and stimulated further discussion through the production of "reply" charts by different groups, putting forward alternative views and interpretations.

Next, further local meetings were held, attended by experts from the various themes and disciplines discussed so that they could register directly the "request for information" that emerged and add their expertise to the preparation of further "reply charts". Finally, a series of "citizens' seminars" took place and exhibitions were held of the "material of cultural self-awareness for the development of the local reality" in each municipality.

Together, these activities led to a series of concrete activities and practical work proposals. In one of the areas for instance, a Centre for Socio-Cultural initiatives was founded and still functions. Agricultural co-operatives were created and other activities connected to the constitution of the consultation centre developed.

The sucess of the whole MOTER project can be seen both in the real activities arising out of it and the unanimous demand by each area concerned for their continuation. The latter demand is particularly significant because it was not a request for the university to continue the project but a recognition that the various local committees must take the initiative and continue the work themselves. There was, in short, an acceptance of local responsibility for the development of their own community. The "self-education" process had really taken off. The exercise had, in the words of its instigator, revealed "the presence of a not indifferent human capital, rich in unsuspected possibilities, that is waiting only to come out of the silence ... to bring new life to an area" (op. cit., p. 44).

3. Discovering entrepreneurship: "Micro-societies"

Entrepreneurship in its various forms and in both private and public sectors is an essential element in many new local development policies, as we have already seen. Entrepreneurship understood as individuals and groups seeing opportunities for action and organising to take advantage of them requires initiative and organising skills, seeking out information and putting together options of different kinds. Above all it means taking an active role in whatever operation is envisaged. A good deal of attention was devoted to this issue at the Venice meeting, much of which is reflected in Dr. George Richmond's paper (Education for Development) which is reproduced here.

The potential for such entrepreneurial initiatives and such an active role is rarely developed by school systems at any level. Traditional teaching methods on the contrary encourage in pupils passive behaviour and reinforce compliance with rewards. While emphasizing the individual rather than the group, they nevertheless define achievement in terms of very narrow limits and on the whole reward it with purely "academic" prestige (grades). Non-conformity is suspect to teachers as likely to undermine class discipline and there are few ways for the less academic to develop their talents, to take initiative and to improve their skills in the organisation of the legitimate activities of their peers. Technical education, even, has normally aimed to provide a child with specific professional skills which he or she will use on the eixsting labour market. Technical school graduates are expected to enter pre-existing slots in employment and are not taught to seek to create their own outlets and opportunities as a context for their technical skills. Still less are they taught to co-operate with their fellows in the creation of such opportunities.

At its least successful, the education system in many countries fails to help pupils realise their entrepreneurial potential, understood in a wide sense. Equally serious, many systems fail to offer many children, in deprived areas in particular, the "traditional" skills that will enable them to be upwardly socially mobile. Many children simply drop out and withdraw from formal education through prolonged truancy (even from the age of 8-10 years) or through sinking into silence and totally passive behaviour as well as more probably disruptive contact. In the following section, Dr. George Richmond draws on his own experience of primary schools in the more difficult areas of New York and describes the successful educational alternative he developed there.

The experiment described has a "private enterprise" referent. There would seem no reason, however, that the principles of the method could not be used with a community focus. Children could then learn the skills which are necessary to entrepreneurial acitivity, both public and private, but recognise that there are different possible value systems and alternative ways of organising productive activity.

EDUCATION FOR DEVELOPMENT: ATTITUDES AND CAPACITIES

by George Richmond,
Director, Private Industry Council, Philadelphia

It is the argument of this paper that schools and training centers that serve the economically disadvantaged should recognise that this population requires a different educative experience than that which they have so far received. It has become increasingly clear that children and youth from particularly badly-off families, those who depend on public welfare, social security and unemployment insurance, or those who are on low wages cannot reach for a more affluent position in society with the knowledge or know-how delivered to them by present education programs. Present programs do not encourage economic autonomy or develop economic behavior appropriate to the situation of the children concerned. The poor, therefore, do not know what steps it may be possible for them to take to get from poverty to relative affluence. Present programming does not teach the poor to be productive. It does not prepare either workers for work or managers to manage. Present education programs appear to be teaching reading, writing and arithmetic over and over again. Children and youth appear to recycle through the education system over and over again to receive larger and larger doses of instruction that will not take.

The reason these doses of instruction do not take hold is that they are disconnected from economic and social reality. In other words, educational services now being offered to the poor have a low utility for them. Because of this low utility, many of the economically disadvantaged do not have the motivation to learn the information or master the cognitive processes professional teachers wish to impart to them. I argue further that the poor have come to the basic conclusion that public education not only plays a marginal role in their personal economic development but also a marginal role in the overall economic development of their community. They appear to be right.

This paper addresses the issue of how make the education, employment and training system in place in a city contribute more directly to the economic development both of the people and of the local community and describes one possible strategy.

In the United States, there has been a perceptible movement in education circles to re-evaluate the role of the school in community economic development and to encourage youth and children to become active participants in economic activity at a very early age.

I am not suggesting that we abandon schools in order to educate our children in our factories or offices. Nor am I suggesting that we create two kinds of educative experience, one for the rich and one for the poor. I am proposing that schools formulate economic development strategies and develop economic development programs in line with the economic development agenda of a city and its people. The strategies needed to accomplish this agenda differ between children and youth, and between youth and adults so they need to be treated separately.

Children in school: Experiments with the creation of a socio-economic system

A schoolroom is a social system. A schoolhouse contains many of these social systems. Although they are social systems, their character is anything but modern. They utilise a primitive system of currency: grades. They have a primitive organization;

teachers behave like manor lords, imposing their rule on children whom they expect to operate as serfs. However, these classroom serfs may not engage in any activity that might be called wealth-producing. Since citizens of classrooms produce no good or service of value to anyone, they have no need for markets or exchanges; therefore, none exist in schools. Children and youth remain in this non-economic milieu for 10 to 12 years - long enough, I fear, to insure that we have to educate them a second time if we desire to see them become wealth producers. While traditional curricula contain information about feudalism, jobs, government, economies, and commerce, educators rarely involve children directly in commercial activity. Despite the near universal acceptance of John Dewey's observation that children learn by doing, and the plentiful signs that children retain the types of information we feed them no longer than a few hours, educators show few signs of redirecting schools to provide "economically disadvantaged" children with the information and know-how they need to free themselves of the "disadvantaged" label. We need to change this result. We have to develop education systems tuned into the economic development needs of children, youth and adults. We need to redirect schools so they contribute to the larger economic development agenda of the community. How can this be done?

In 1967, I led a small experiment in a school serving children from an impoverished neighborhood in Brooklyn, New York. I wanted to see if I could generate a commercial revolution of their feudal society. To make this change I introduced some of the factors of economic development into the social system of my 5th grade classroom. These factors included: (1) money, (2) various forms of property, (3) markets or exchanges, and (4) economic organizations. For various reasons, many of them good, these ingredients have never been part of the educative process in a country like mine where these factors dominate adult experience. I began by printing paper currency. I created a classroom store and financed its inventory out of my own pocket. The goods in the store could be purchased with the paper currency or "micro-dollars" that I printed. Students worked to obtain these micro-dollars. In imitation of our national employment policy, I created jobs and established wage rates for each job. The jobs were simple at first: custodian, secretary, board-washer, politician and monitor. They grew more complex when I devised and introduced a real estate simulation. The simulation generated jobs for real estate managers and brokers, cashiers, transportation managers, contractors, architects, surveyors, accountants and related occupations.

Probably the most dramatic individual development in this Micro-Economy was the development of a bank by Ramon Hernandez. Ten-year-old Ramon was a weak, frail and shy individual. He had, however, one talent no one in the class possessed. He could add and subtract. These talents made Ramon a member of its intellectual elite. Sometimes he could even multiply. His arithmetic ability made him a natural choice to be banker. As many realise, banks function some place near the center of most economic activity, and bankers as a consequence, often play central roles in our social system. Such was the case with Ramon. Shy, puny Ramon, once on the fringes of classroom dominated by his more muscular peers, moved to the center of things. He became the dominant force in economic life.

In this and in succeeding demonstrations, the traditional classroom underwent similar transformations. These transformations were concrete as well as historical. We no longer read to learn how to read. We read to use: contracts, deeds, letters, manuscripts, newspapers, and even books produced in our miniature economy. Children learned that reading was necessary if they wanted to survive in their more modern commercial micro-society. In other words, children read for utilitarian reasons. We did not have to force feed children abstract arithmetic concepts when they learned maths willingly and enthusiastically when mathematical concepts were imparted to them through economic development activity. For example, we asked students to do accounting, to make construction estimates, and to use checkbooks, credit cards, budgets and to compute taxes. We taught children arithmetic techniques to accomplish these purposes.

It is important to remember, especially in the current educational climate of increased demand for a "return to basics" that while education in the basics of literacy is a virtual necessity for children and adults contemplating entering the productive workforce, being literate itself does not qualify one to participate in local or even personal economic development strategies. People do not start, maintain, manage or expand businesses and other organisations because they are literate. People engage in economic development activity because they know how. These techniques need to be learned through experience. The Micro-Economic model makes this kind of experience available to children from an early age. Entrepreneurs and managers are provided with ample opportunity to uncover themselves. Cities that want to expand the number of jobs in the local economy are well advised to invest resources in the development of a cadre of entrepreneurs who have learned, by trial and error, to start business ventures or community enterprises and make them work. These youths will become future economic leaders as well as seasoned workers.

In the demonstrations we have run, children 6-12 have developed a variety of small business organizations based in their schools. These have included: banks, bakeries, retail stores, factories, galleries, bookstores, sanitation service companies, law firms, accounting firms, construction companies, tax service agencies, movie-making companies, carnival organisers, fortune tellers, messenger services, photographers, theatre companies, dance companies, and so on. To govern their economic activity, children have developed legislatures, courts and other government agencies. These organizations belong to the long list of institutions children can generate as part of both educative and economic development activity. The lessons of this experience contain many of the ingredients of an educative strategy designed to prepare economically developed people willing and able to develop their communities.

Educational gains

Although the experience in these enterprises may provide an invaluable aid to instructional strategies focusing on literacy, micro-economic experience has the additional advantage of (1) preparing children to work both as employers and employees, and of (2) preparing children to work co-operatively in organizations. Any imaginable strategy for educating people to participate in a community economic development strategy must incorporate these functions, because economic development involves many people working together toward a single result.

What have been the results of micro-economic activity? Some have related to strictly traditional educational goals. In one classroom in Hartford, children registered reading and mathematics gains of two years after six months of the program run in association with other instructional strategies. Similar projects in New York yielded dramatic improvements in reading and maths scores. Others relate to more general aims - understanding the importance of learning and acquiring appropriate values. Perhaps as important, children have seemed more motivated to attend school and while there they more willingly engage themselves in utilitarian educative experiences than they do in the more abstract forms that have little attraction for them.

From these experiences, we conclude that children can and should engage in economic and community development activity from the time they enter school. Not only can it be done, it can be done cheaply, at little or no additional cost. Communities can and need to devise schools that contribute to community economic development.

The demonstrations, as far as they go, can be replicated. What is needed, however, is a rather substantial investment in the development of materials to help deepen the understandings and skills of children engaging in real economic development activity. These curricula should include programs in accounting, law-making and rule administration, and instruction materials on organizational management techniques. We need books or visual materials that introduce real estate, investment, law, construction, architecture, credit, contracts, banking and commerce to children at every age level. Few materials exist that guide students who become engaged in formulating activities relating to government, taxation, structures, municipal budgets, small business enterprises or wages and price schemes.

We also suffer from a shortage of skilled instructors capable of teaching economic development to the disadvantaged. Teachers who do not have this training and orientation cannot be expected to prepare children to discard their "disadvantaged" labels. We need nationally or internationally funded efforts to develop materials for economic development education. We need to train staff to help children use these materials in didactic ways. (Dr. Richmond's contribution concludes at this point.)

B. INTERACTING WITH THE LOCAL COMMUNITY: AN ACTIVE APPROACH TO INDIVIDUAL LEARNING AND COMMUNITY IMPROVEMENT

The experiments described above illustrate the importance of schools and institutions of adult education being concerned to produce knowledge about their local environment and in the process teach both children and local residents the tools with which to analyse their situation. We now proceed from there to draw together innovatory schemes operating in a variety of Member countries which address the problem of local development through community service at the same time as they help individual students choose careers. The focus is on learning through doing. It is on schemes that involve young people in the real activities of public agencies and thus to contribute to the welfare of their community at the same time as they gain the academic credits necessary for pursuing their own education at the next stage. Some of these schemes operate in schools, others with school-leavers, and others with adults. More of them link together both aspects of education and development through linking the indirect and direct roles educational institutions can play in the development of local areas, understood in the sense of the improvement of local conditions. We here emphasize the public sector activities children and youth can be involved with and the community service orientation of the programme is to the fore. Here, too, "entrepreneurship", understood in its widest sense, can be as important as it is to a more strictly economic development which is the focus of the next part of this report.

1. Community involvement programmes

Programmes such as those described here are of special interest because they involve not only children and young people from the most deprived sections of their respective societies, but also those who do not suffer such handicaps. They suggest that all young people can potentially benefit from developing themselves and their talents in joint in-school-extra-school activities and that the benefits they gain as people flow on to improve relationships with their families, their peers and others around them. The schemes described are all based on the principle that young people learn better by being able to see that their efforts are of real value to other people, that what they do does make a real difference to others. The students become more motivated, retain information more effectively and are more able to co-operate with others. The programmes thus benefit both children and community.

One course of this kind has been running successfully for some years in the province of Ontario in Canada. In several places there, young people in secondary schools are able to earn academic course credits for spending part of their time as volunteers in local social service agencies. Each course is composed of three parts: in-school classes, an independent study project and a fixed period of hours in an agency in the social service sector of the community. The scheme is entered on a voluntary basis by the students, so motivation is high. The students are usually aged between 16 and 18 years and are in grade 12. The course carries about one half of their academic credit for that grade. Participants come from a range of academic programmes - terminal high school vocationally oriented programmes, those intending to go to community college and university bound students. They are principally girls and come from a broad range of socio-economic backgrounds.

Students work in day-care centres, classes for handicapped children and adults, police departments, welfare and probation agencies, museums and newspaper and community television channels amongst others. They work at least 10 hours a week for the entire year and perform jobs jointly worked out between their supervisors in the agency, their teachers and themselves. They spend three hours a week in classes taught by the Community Involvement teacher and also carry out an independent study project on an issue related to their work or community issues more generally. The results of the programme are highly encouraging, both on the individual side and on the agency side and although it is designed primarily with an orientation to the <u>students</u>, the agencies and hence the community also benefit. Some staff in the schools, usually those whose students are not principally in the CIP scheme, found it difficult to organise their timetables and some students found it difficult on occasion to return to class after periods in the agencies as they experienced the differences in type of work and activity required. But the scheme was clearly positive overall. Professor David Brison, the originator of the programme, which has been favourably evaluated several times, and is running in several schools, reports that:

> "the programme has a marked impact on the students enrolled. The most visible impact is ... maturation - students take more responsibility for their own actions, have more social poise, are more tolerant of others, are able to deal more effectively in situations where there is social conflict and feel better about themselves. Their parents also report that they are easier to live with. In other areas, they have learned how their communities are organised to deal with local problems and there is some evidence that they are more alert to issues in their communities." (Brison, 1978).

Teachers, parents and students themselves all reported improvements.

The programme also had benefits in that it assisted the students with making long-term career choices and in giving them real understanding of the world of work. Career choices became clearer; more than two-thirds of those involved reported that the scheme had influenced them. The students felt also more committed to their decisions. Through the course, too, its graduates gain advantage in entry to community colleges and in obtaining jobs in the social service sector (Usher, 1977, passim). This was seen in interviews and surveys which indicated that more than 50 per cent of the Community Involvement Programme (CIP) students continued to work on a voluntary basis in the agencies to which they had been assigned after the termination of the project or academic course year (op. cit., p. 12). Finally, student satisfaction with the programme can be seen by the fact that virtually all said that they would have taken the course even as a non-credit course if they had had the time.

Similar programmes also operate in the United States where early high school dropping-out is a major problem, in poor areas of cities in particular. Each programme varies in emphasis but a New York example indicates possibilities. For more than a decade now, in response to an accelerating high school drop-out rate, increasing unemployment and the many social problems that face young people, New York State has been implementing a programme aimed at maintaining students in school while providing job training opportunities.

The scheme, known as the Youth Opportunity Program, was originally sponsored by the New York State Department of Mental Hygiene and it is administered in hospitals around the State. Students, on the basis of their own preferences, are assigned to clinical, support or clerical positions and spend normally two years on the programme, until they graduate. Each participant is evaluated by a supervisor every three months and counselled on improvement strategies where necessary.

Again the results are encouraging. Programme participants are much more likely than the state average to graduate from high school in spite of their concentration in low-income families. Similarly, almost half go on to technical or college education. The scheme allows these students to develop motivation for learning and to acquire real work experience (almost two years) by the time they graduate from high school. They can thus face their future with both better academic qualifications and work skills than would otherwise have been possible. In the words of evaluators of the scheme, "the linking of academic education with actual work experience provides students with the opportunity to realise the applied importance of academic subject matter to ... work experience ... it enables them to integrate their academic knowledge with everyday job requirements" (Pena et al., 1979). The community has gained too; not only have the hospitals gained manpower but also an improved image in the types of local residents who can begin to see the important role of the hospital as a community agency (op. cit.).

In Europe, too, innovatory schemes linking the training of young people in school to the improvement of life conditions of local residents are beginning to appear. Even in countries where education is largely centrally directed, such as Italy, ways are being found of getting young people still at school out into their local communities.

In Italy, the city of Bologna education authorities have begun to experiment with schemes for technical school students. There, it is felt that while a comprehensive reform may be necessary, some indications of methods to use for it and appropriate studies in that direction may be derived from local initiatives taken in response to specific real situations.

Two prongs of action were chosen. One involved research into labour markets and will be described in a later section of this report. The second involved experiments in combined academic studies and practical experience. These were varied. Some involved work experience during the term and in the summer vacations for students still in training; others involved the admission of people at work to courses at the technical school, either on "sandwich" courses or on "150 hour" (the employment training act 150 hours) crash courses for late learners or short seminars.

The aim of the scheme was to introduce students to forms of socially useful work, as suggested in proposed national legislation, and to improve their understanding of labour and its organisation. The scheme had two parts, a practical and a theoretical. In the practical component, students left the school and went out to work on a community project. In the institute concerned, all the members of a fifth year class specialising in the building trades have been allocated four hours a week to work on a building site leased by the City Council to a building co-operative, Manutecoop. The work place was chosen to be of social importance; it was an old country house, listed as an historical monument, being converted to become a centre of social services, on the one hand for the aged and on the other for the very young. The site offered a wide variety of training possibilities in the different building trades while at the same time it provided the occasion for students to reflect on local urban improvement policies. It thus was a means of achieving potentially closer links between education and local development. It will now be extended to provide opportunities as well for historical research on the town's buildings and provide the basis for more academic historical and geographical courses as well as a means of understanding the shape of the present city.

The second part of the project was also innovatory. It involved bringing together experts from different organisations and disciplines to encourage a greater understanding of the whole construction industry and a better linking of theory and practice in the field. This was done in seminars conducted within the school. The themes covered involved: the role of construction in reconstruction; relations between town and district and problems relating to urban policy; housing needs in Italy; the organisation of work in the construction industry; the building cycle and new building techniques; building legislation and conditions and opportunities for work in the industry. Thus it can be seen that an attempt was made to cover not only the industrial techniques themselves but also the context of the industry and local policies and situations that bear on it.

An Italian evaluation reported that the project was, in spite of many difficulties, an undoubted success. The results represent a synthesis of the efforts of a number of groups; the local authority, the collegiate bodies of the school, the students themselves, as active and alert individuals with a notable capacity for being critical of the problem of work and organised labour, the trade union which, "realising that training problems are closely interconnected with those inherent in the productive process and improved labour organisation has encouraged to the utmost the mingling of students and operatives and consistently supported the experiment". Local evaluators concluded that the project was extremely valuable in a number of ways. First, it created real relationships between local workers and young people, and positive attitudes towards their work on the part of the students. Second, it opened new perspectives for solving middle management supply problems in the industry. Thirdly, it helped bring the teachers up to date with their discipline. Finally, and this is especially important, the work of the young people concerned was notably better on the site than in schools and their motivation much stronger.

In another experiment in the same city, eighty young people from the first and second years of study in mechanical engineering, electronics and building from Aldini-Valeriani Institute worked on local sites run by co-operatives and in local engineering firms. This particular experiment was chosen because the casual work students usually did in the holidays had no relation to the profession they were studying for and made a break with school.

The summer work periods were approximately forty days. The students in companies were paid "bursaries", partly provided by the firms and partly by a local social services fund for workmen. The latter was the result of an agreement between the trade unions and the employers' associations. The co-operatives paid the entire "wages" of the students. The work experience was planned to maximise the educational content being closely related to the jobs students were studying for and the students, often working in co-operatives, gained experience of "alternative" forms of productive enterprise and their organisation, while at the same time improving the local community amenities. As a result, the experiment may now be expanded to term-time activities and to other disciplines.

A similar experiment was also reported to the Venice Colloquium by Belgian participants. In a suburb of Brussels, a technical school has recently bought an old semi-derelict house in the country and this has been completely renovated by its students for use as a holiday house - both for the students themselves and for other local children who would otherwise be unable to leave the city on holiday. The students thus were able to learn their trades while producing a product of real value to themselves and to the less fortunate members of their community.

This scheme has parallels with a Canadian experiment. There, technical students in Ontario city schools developed links with their rural counterparts and together built holiday accommodation for city children from deprived areas so that they could holiday in and learn about the countryside around their city.

One final scheme is worthy of mention here: although its location is in a third world city, it may well be of relevance to the problems of cities in the OECD countries. The experiment was devised in Mexico for 11-14-year-olds in the most deprived urban areas who have, to all intents and purposes, dropped out from school. In this, school timetables are adjusted so as to enable children to mix in-school activities with outside ones, the latter being linked to the concern of the local community, notably health. One thing they have done within the "11-14 system" is to develop a programme of preventive medicine by finding out which local children have not been vaccinated and then going to see the parents to persuade them to get this done. They also keep health records in this sort of field.

In other countries more direct attempts are made at community education per se. In Britain, in many cities there are numbers of initiatives in this direction, there being an increasing number of community organisations willing to provide help for schools in their development of a social education curriculum. While some contribute materials to an "environmental education" course of the kind already described, others, such as the Manchester Youth and Community Service, aim "to act as an advisory and support service to schools which are planning to develop community education programmes which include <u>an element of practical involvement in problem situations outside school</u>" (P. Jones, 1978, p. 77, our emphasis). One group has, for example, designed and built a Wendy house commissioned by a local playgroup leader, has made a videotape on child development for a lecturer at a nearby college, and has carried out a survey of pre-school provision in the area.

In contrast, however, to the schemes described above, the British schemes are not institutionalised with links between particular agencies or disciplines and do not consistently form part of a course recognised for academic credit. Although in some cases, projects undertaken contribute to CSE or 'O' level examination work, this is usually on an ad hoc basis.

It would seem that a serious commitment to "alternation" schemes which include both in-school and extra-school activities requires that these be made part of recognised courses in a consistent manner. If this is not done, there is a tendency for staff to send only "non-academic" pupils who will not be entered for examinations. In that case, community involvement work is downgraded to a matter of "only doing useful jobs". We will return to this in a final section of the report.

2. <u>Housing, environment and welfare improvement: Programmes for inner-city youth</u>

Community involvement programmes operating in school frequently encourage young people to stay on at school or to enter further or higher education in preparation for entry to a particular career. Many other young people, however, do in fact leave school at the earliest possible date and do so without having acquired formal qualifications of any kind. These are the adolescents at greatest risk of either prolonged unemployment, with all the attendant ills, or unstable employment in dead-end and ill-paid jobs, often themselves leading back to long-term unemployment at a later date.

Programmes for these young people play an especial part in realising the potential of local residents in a way that could be harnessed both to their personal advantage and to the development of their local communities. There is a myriad of such schemes in operation in OECD countries, although the great majority would certainly be found in North America and then the United Kingdom. Many are run by Departments of Labour or their equivalents rather than by Ministries of Education but they are important here because they combine training programmes with opportunities for young people to contribute real improvements to their local environment and the conditions of life of local residents. Successful programmes, then, provide young people with a series of skills relevant to the opportunities of their local areas and at the same time provide a context within which they can develop their own sense of personal contribution through co-operating in common activities with others.

3. Housing rehabilitation

One of the fields in which many of these training-cum-work programmes for out-of-school young people are applied is housing rehabilitation. In the United States, CETA (Comprehensive Employment and Training Act) funds from the Department of Labor can be combined with monies provided by other federal agencies, such as the Department of Housing and Urban Development (HUD) or the Economic Development Agency (EDA), and their State and local counterparts to finance such projects. There are many variations about the way they are used in practice.

One example is provided by a project known as Banana Kelly in New York's devastated South Bronx. Here an architect from the Pratt Insitute in Brooklyn provides the technical assistance necessary to help a group of local high school drop-outs rehabilitate a row of abandoned but large houses. Twenty young people, supervised by a community worker and local tradesmen designated by the trade unions of the building trade learn the different skills involved in planning and reconstructing property. At weekends they are joined by the future residents of the apartments who work with them under the New York Sweat Equity scheme for urban homesteading. The youngsters concerned participate in each aspect of the construction, ultimately specialising in one trade. They learn not only the technical skills but also the social skills needed for a community-oriented project and, frequently the hard way, they learn the importance of precision and order in work and the reasons behind the technical methods they are learning (if you do things in the wrong order, the roof collapses, as indeed one had on the Banana Kelly site). In study sessions on site and after work, they learn the theoretical knowledge required but also how to get the funding required, the drawing up of project proposals, how to approach and deal with local urban authorities, the exigencies of arguing cases cogently and effectively. These are all skills they will need, not only in working on housing projects, but also in their everyday dealings with public and private agencies and with potential employers.

Turnover of membership in such groups is high but it must be remembered that the clients of such projects are young people who bear all the hallmarks of a childhood spent in acute urban poverty. In many such areas, too, there are links between schemes; in some, for instance, young people are being mobilised to work on weatherising schemes, energy conservation projects, and other aspects of urban homesteading.

Another New York group, this time in East Harlem, composed largely of minority youth, often ex-drug addicts and ex-convicts, has gone beyond the housing rehabilitation schemes on which it began to propose a whole local economic development plan. Realising that improving housing is not the whole answer to neighbourhood revitalisation in areas which have degenerated so far, such groups are putting up plans for the encouragement of local commerce and manufacturing, both in the private sector and through the creation of production and service co-operatives.

Similar initiatives are evolving in Europe. In Kreuzberg, for instance, an area of Berlin inhabited principally by Gastarbeiter from Turkey and southern Europe, local groups are working with people from the technical university in schemes to improve both the physical surroundings that people live in and the training and chances of employment of the community's young people. In France, too, a number of community enterprises have been created or are in the process of creation in different cities and many of these concentrate on housing rehabilitation, as for instance, in Grenoble. The training functions of these are not always as explicit and formalised as they are in the American models, partly because the system of funding is so different, but participation in such projects is a combination of learning-by-doing that could be taken up and deepened in conjunction with local educators drawn from a variety of institutions.

In Adelaide, South Australia's major city, there also now exist a number of innovative projects for out-of-school but unemployed youth which are linking training to activities that benefit the local community. Project CITY (Community Improvement Through Youth) provides its clients with advice and counselling on a wide variety of matters but also organises training camps, workshops and seminars to develop new and improved existing individual skills. Equally important, the CITY scheme gives grants to youth under the age of 25 to initiate community improvement projects which they can run themselves with appropriate support. In Melbourne, too, the Departments concerned with Labour and Youth Affairs have initiated a series of similar projects.

In sum, these programmes all have a set of common aims. They seek, through education, training and the provision of opportunities to put new or improved skills to constructive use in the interests both of the individual young people concerned and their local community to develop and utilise to a maximum the human resources which so often in our societies go to waste. More specifically, as Brison wrote of the Canadian experiments, they seek to help students contribute at one and the same time to the solution of their own and their community's social problems. They thus seek:

- to generate knowledge, derived from practical experience, of problems at community level;

- to develop a commitment to the solution of these problems;

- to gain the skills needed for their solution.

At the same time, these programmes develop individual professional skills, knowledge of group processes and analytical skills and through this combination seek to build up young people's confidence in themselves as actors involved in constructive and valuable activities. The construction of this "developed" person is a major step in the development of an area's human resources. The next step is to find productive outlets for the energy released, in both private and non-profit or public sections. Education's contribution to that step is the subject of our next part.

Part Three

EDUCATION'S ROLE IN ECONOMIC DEVELOPMENT

As the Renegades of East Harlem discovered by experience, housing rehabilitation and even the improved provision of community services is not enough: for once better housed and better cared-for, the residents of rundown urban areas also need jobs. Their adolescent and young adult children also need jobs. Economic revitalisation has to be the basis for the long-term welfare of local urban communities. The return, maintenance or expansion of productive activities is the sine qua non of a functioning neighbourhood or locality. The education system, both formal and non-formal, both in-school and post-school, can make significant contributions both to the maintenance of the existing productive base so as to prevent further decline and to the creation of further economic activities. This part of the report traces a variety of areas, projects and schemes in which different kinds of educational provision are concerned, more or less directly, with the improvement of the economic development of local urban communities.

If these new initiatives are to be effective, then education for entrepreneurship cannot start too early. In a very few places, there have been experiments with it at primary school level. Most of these have been in the United States (Hartford, San Jose, Los Angeles) and aimed at encouraging children aged between 6 and 11 years to produce goods and services of value to other children or to the greater community. One such experiment has been described above.

Most such training, however, occurs within secondary and especially in upper secondary schools. There are two main ways of approaching training for entrepreneurship at that level in an active way. The first, and in some ways more radical, method involves giving young people still in school the opportunity to run their own businesses based in the school. The second approach involves school class groups in consulting activities at the request of local businesses, whether industrial or commercial. Both are discussed below.

Post-secondary institutions also have a responsibility in the field and a section in this part of the present report discusses what needs to be done and brings together innovations in the field.

A. SECONDARY EDUCATION AND ENTERPRISE

A report in 1978 by Youthaid, in Britain, a major agency concerned with the problems of youth employment and unemployment, showed that "it was not the supposed traumas of entering work which worried young people; on the contrary, it was the realistic fear of not entering work at all" (Study of the Transition from School to Working Life, Youthaid, London, 1978). 'Success in getting a job, the same study reported, depended more on the number of jobs available in the area than it did on qualifications. In some areas, more than 80 per cent of school-leavers had been unemployed for some period and in Liverpool more than 50 per cent of any cohort of school-leavers were unemployed for many months. Other OECD Member countries include cities where the situation is similar (OECD, 1980a). It is thus not sufficient simply to provide more training; the aim of education for development even in secondary schools must also be to provide more jobs. In this domain it seems to be increasingly recognised by policy-makers that unfortunately:

"Self-employment and entrepreneurship both as an idea and strategy for dealing with the problems of youth have not received the attention they deserve from youth planners, youth workers or youth leaders themselves. Ever since youth has been regarded as a subject for development, attempts in dealing with youth an an important manpower resource for development or as problems that have to be immediately met are evolving around such subjects like the role of youth in national youth development, youth and unemployment, youth in community service, youth and vocational training and other similar subjects which provide discussion at a philosophical and theoretical level, at the level of identification of related problems or defining roles for youths. It is only very recently that self-employment and even more recently the promotion of entrepreneurship among youth have received some attention." (A. Amad, "Infrastructure for Promoting Self Employment and Entrepreneurship" in Commonwealth Secretariat, Youth in Business, London, 1978, p. 25, our emphasis.)

Efforts in many countries are now being made to remedy this.

1. School-based youth enterprises

A number of OECD countries have begun to experiment with initiatives involving young people in schools producing real goods and in running their own enterprises associated with the production and marketing of these real products. The schemes vary in the amount of time pupils spend in these activities. Where they operate in the general education parts of secondary schools, the amount of time spent on them per week is relatively small. In the technical streams of high schools, however, much, if not all, of the training concerned may be carried out in relation to a particular enterprise. In the former set of schemes, the aim is the apprenticeship of entrepreneurship per se; in the latter, the principal aim is training in a technical skill (such as mechanical engineering) with which experience of entrepreneurship is associated. In the latter cases, too, the enterprises will last over a longer period of time, taking in successive generations of students, and ploughing profits back into expansion of the enterprise or the creation or development of associated enterprises within the same school or school system. In the former case, in contrast, each enterprise is usually linked to the year a group of students spends in any one grade. The general entrepreneurship learning model may find easier acceptance in schools, at least at present, for it involves less fundamental reorganisation of timetables, teaching methods and teacher training, and so on.

Taking "general entrepreneurship education" first: several OECD Member countries are running such schemes. Two currently operating in Great Britain may be used to illustrate them. "Youth Enterprise", started by a merchant banker on the American "Junior Achievement" model, is now operating in 3,000 secondary schools in Britain. It is run as a non-profit-making charity and is dependent on funds provided by industry and commerce.

"Young Enterprise" aims to provide school students with the opportunity of learning about the organisation, management and operation of a business by forming and running their own miniature company for one year. With the help of a "Young Enterprise" kit and advisers from a local company, the students take on the roles necessary for the formation and running of a company. They hold board meetings, decide upon a product, raise capital by selling shares, buy the raw materials and manufacture and sell their product. The group does all the paperwork and after 9 months produces a report and balance sheet and distributes any dividend to shareholders. As part of the scheme, regional competitions are held for participating schools and firms.

A second British scheme was started in Northumberland schools in 1978. The School-Production Experience Project (SPEX) aims to give every pupil in the participating school the opportunity to experience at first hand the processes and problems encountered in designing, producing and marketing an article to an acceptable standard. This project is of much shorter duration (one week) and, while a start, may need considerable extension if it is to be real training for entrepreneurship by young people. (Information provided by the United Kingdom Report for the ELD Project, Spring 1980.)

Some countries run such projects specifically for young people who have remained at school because they were unable to find employment. In such schemes, greater space in the timetable is given to entrepreneurial training, which may be the principal area of study, supplemented by only one or two of the more academic disciplines.

At least one such experimental scheme has been launched in Australia, in Fern Tree Gully, a suburb of Melbourne. The Industry Programme in 1980 involved 15-20 students from years 11 and 12 (the final years of high school). The primary aim is to help students gain employment in areas they have themselves identified or, should that be unattainable, to provide them with viable alternatives both within the traditional workforce and outside it. The scheme sets out to develop the both practical and social and personal skills and involves co-operation among the group's members in common activity as well as the involvement of people outside the school, some giving advice and teaching skills, others from community groups with whom it is hoped that the students will develop working relationships.

The Industry Program is run along the lines of a small business set up to service schools and the community. The enterprise constructs simple equipment for schools and contracts to do small building and maintenance jobs for schools or people in the community. A retired accountant teaches the students an accounting system by which all transactions are controlled and analysed. Students spend 12 periods of 50 minutes each week on industry and study in addition English and two elective subjects. Two teachers conduct the course and a third provides some administrative help. (Information provided by the Australian Commonwealth Education Department, Canberra, in the Australian country report for the ELD Project, October 1980.)

In the United States, too, such initiatives are widespread. Many of the major cities (and some rural areas too) have begun in-school schemes of youth enterprises. Many of them depart from the European model in that they provide wages or other forms of remuneration to students who work on them. In Saint-Paul, Minnesota, for example, the Public Schools have inaugurated six projects which young people in the schools manage and staff. The students first set up a personnel office, which receives requests for services from within the school system and arranges for students to perform these duties for pay. Students also manage a graphic arts studio, a performing-arts group, a construction action centre and a consumer centre (Youthwork, an Overview, 1979, p. 29).

Other American high schools are using in-school youth enterprises on a larger scale as a teaching-mechanism in Education for Economic Development programmes. One of the most advanced is that of Mesa Verde High School in California. That school has reorganised much of its teaching and learning procedures in enterprise forms. Teachers hired for their entrepreneurial bent join with groups of high school students to form a company. Each company produces a good or service that it sells. Each company provides owners and members with employment at wages that vary with the revenue generated by the businesses. About 20 businesses run at any one time and include products such as pottery, films, food, wood and plastic products and a newspaper. Interestingly, too, they also produce curriculum material for elementary schools, custodial services for the school and management consulting services. There is also a loan company and a student-run restaurant instead of the canteen (Richmond, 1975, para. 4.4).

In this way, each company provided high school students with "direct organisational experience, demanded disciplined co-operation in the production of goods that would go to market to draw funds that would eventually cover the cost of goods sold, the costs of borrowing and the cost of wages for students in each business" (ibid.). In addition to this the students were involved in community and self-development. By building their own infrastructure they learned at first hand a wide variety of skills needed both in working life and community activities.

The most radical departure into this field, however, seems to have been undertaken by the Hartford Public Schools in Connecticut in conjunction with the local Chamber of Commerce. The Hartford schemes are described in the paper immediately following as an illustration of how, in practice, school-based youth enterprises may function.

There are few directly comparable schemes in Europe. One which has been set up in a purely experimental manner has now been operating since 1977 in Montluçon in France. Aiming to teach the skills of business management, two sections (boiler-making and smelting) of a Montluçon technical lycée have been adapted to function as enterprises. In these two sections, students design, manufacture and sell a product, aided and supervised by specialist teachers. As the programme is highly experimental and involves adapting the official curriculum of the subjects by local teachers, only one hour a week over two academic years is presently devoted to the scheme as such although technical problems associated with the production side are discussed and dealt with in workshop hours. It seems that it will, however, be developed further and run over a longer period ("Comment créer son entreprise", Avenirs, 1980, pp. 43-44).

2. Youth in-school enterprises in Hartford
(contributed by Dr. George Richmond)

During the last four years, the United States, through the Department of Labor, has invested billions of dollars in an attempt to solve a serious youth unemployment problem. Some of us have taken advantage of this investment to extend the education for economic development agenda described above from children to youth.

In the City of Hartford, Connecticut, I recently had the fortune of designing a large-scale youth employment project. One of the primary features of this project was the generation of a set of school-based enterprises. These enterprises produce goods and services and bring them to market; they also provide youth with the opportunities to develop marketable skills. This dual agenda occasioned the invention of a new term to describe a business enterprise that produces both goods and services and trained workers. We call such enterprises "training ventures". During our first three years in Hartford we launched three major enterprises, and a half-dozen smaller ones. Among these were an auto repair venture, a graphics and printing venture, a loan company, and a typing and copy service. Of these, perhaps the auto venture has been the most impressive. Initiated before my arrival, the additional resources obtained from the President's Youth initiatives aided the maturation and expansion of the enterprise.

The basic business of the auto center is a repair service. Students work under the direction of a team of teachers who supervise their training and the transition they make to unsubsidized unemployment at the completion of training. Students do the work. The auto center, a regular business, repairs approximately 75 cars a year in its auto body shop and another 200 cars in its motor repair division. About 50 per cent of the center's market consists of teachers and other school personnel. The remaining 50 per cent of the center's business comes from the general public. The center does about $60,000 worth of business each year.

The school-based enterprises do not compete unfairly with local business and can even be beneficial to it as the following example shows. Following my arrival in Hartford, we invested additional resources in the center's expansion into two new lucrative activities. The first was a Used Car Preparation and Sales dealership. The center now purchases used cars, repairs and refurbishes them, and then sells them at an auction. The second new activity links the school to a local private business as a sub-contractor. A private concern in town decided it wanted to get out of the alternator and generator repair field because it did not have sufficient demand for that service to sustain a full-time staff. The auto center offered to set up the business as one of its activities. The lower operating costs of the school system made the activity profitable for it. When the businessman offered to transfer his facilities to the school system and to sub-contract the work he needed done to it, we accepted.

A printing, copying and advertising training venture called Graphica found its Hartford market in another way. It developed demand for its services among non-profit agencies in Hartford devoted to youth. The school system itself contracted a portion of its business to Graphica. One of the printers lured to the staff of Graphica added his network of past customers to their market.

The methods by which the enterprises were set up were successful and could be copied elsewhere. For both the auto venture and Graphica, the school system employed entrepreneurs to establish the venture. The entrepreneur hired and supervised an experienced production staff and an experienced training staff. Both production and training people shared both responsibilities, and youth were trained in all aspects of business development. Youth with entrepreneurial interests or management skills graduated with marketable skills and with a knowledge of small venture development. One student in the auto venture put this knowledge to work immediately. He purchased a set of tools and started his own auto repair and tune-up business after school hours; he reportedly grossed as much as $1,000 per month on his own.

This model may be a useful one to people interested in encouraging schools to participate more directly in economic development activity. Essentially we based our ventures on the existing capital resources of the school system. A business that starts with reduced costs for facilities, heat, light, telephone and personnel is at a distinct advantage in the marketplace when compared with business entities that must plow working capital into these factors before production can start. For most training ventures, the costs of constant staff turnover and retraining are more than offset by these direct operating subsidies to the business.

There are difficulties, however. The more serious obstacles to school-based business development are: 1) scheduling; 2) labor agreements that restrict the normal length of the work day to six hours; 3) certification procedures that inhibit business enterprises from attracting managers and teachers from outside education circles; and 4) obtaining investment capital.

In Hartford we overcame all of them. We overcame the timetabling obstacle by starting an independently scheduled two-shift school called Workplaces. One group of students worked in the morning and took academic courses in the afternoon. A second group followed an afternoon work and morning academic schedule. The business ventures we developed were able to draw on both of these groups for their student workforce. The second obstacle, a teacher labor agreement limiting instructors to a five-hour work day, and an eight-month academic year, was altered through negotiations with the Teachers' Union. Eager to attract new federal resources and jobs to the school system, the Hartford Federation of Teachers agreed to an 8-hour day, 12-month year at a market rate. Under a formula spelled out by the Labor agreement, each new job receives three bids from the employers outside the school system. These bids are average to obtain a teacher's starting wage and only then does the employee hook into the other features of the teacher agreement.

Once the starting wage has been established, the salary is plugged into the appropriate step in the teacher agreement. The upshot of this arrangement is that Hartford's ventures may hire 8-hour a day, 12-month year instructors and work supervisors at the prevailing wage. Ventures can operate on a regular business day and year. The schools can remain open longer to make the additional education investments that always need to be made where their clientele is composed of the economically disadvantaged.

The third obstacle, certification, was overcome through the combined resolutions of the Connecticut State Board of Education and the Hartford Board of Education. Both Boards agreed to waive certification requirements for teachers and administrators for a five-year demonstration period during which staff in the school system would evolve certification standards for both administrators and teachers employed in youth employment and training programs.

A fourth frequent obstacle to developing school-based enterprise is the arcane local system of financial disbursements and controls, but this too can be overcome. In Hartford, all disbursements have to be approved by the school system's division of financial control and then by a similar division at City Hall. The minimum time it takes to pay a vendor is three months. One can hardly operate a business under these circumstances. Through the visionary leadership of Hartford city officials, the City Council voted to allow the school district to set up a revolving fund. While the revolving fund is subject to audits by both the school system and by City Hall, each venture manager now has the power to commit his enterprise financially. Hartford ventures pay their vendors and receive payment from their customers without interference or participation in the regular financial disbursement system of the city or the school system. This assures a steady flow of funds in and out of the venture.

These modifications in the logic of a school system took three years to achieve. My intention here is to highlight those factors that one must deal with if one seriously wishes to join the effort to redirect schools into community economic development activity. (This concludes Dr. Richmond's communication.)

3. School-business consulting activities

Some OECD countries are moving towards giving young people in technical and vocational schools the opportunity to put their newly found skills to use in the solving of real problems found in the production process in companies outside. This involves creating close links between the schools and the local enterprises that use their consulting service.

In Norway, for instance, a consulting scheme has been operating for some years in which commercial and industrial upper-secondary schools help solve problems brought to them by companies as a major part of their learning process. In these schemes, the students of each school "do not spend much of their time reading textbooks or solving problems from some learning programme, nor in listening to lectures". Instead, most of their learning tasks come from local industry and function through "consulting". Companies inform the teachers of problems arising in their production process. Students and teacher then visit the plant concerned, gather data on equipment and problem and work in groups in the school laboratory on finding a solution which is then tried out in the plant itself. The programme seems to benefit staff, who keep up to date with real production situations, who gain knowledge of these situations, and industry, which acquires cheap advice on an individualised basis (Blichfeldt, 1975).

In France, too, similar schemes have long been running in certain parts of the technical system of education and particularly in the ORT schools, now often especially concerned with immigrant children.

B. LINKING WORK AND EDUCATION FOR DEVELOPMENT

1. Youth enterprise and training outside school

Youth enterprises created and working outside the formal school system often have an important component; training programmes which aim both to develop the specific skills of the participants and their entrepreneurial abilities. Many of these are linked to different parts of the formal education system. These often provide in effect alternative forms of schooling for young people who have been unable to work successfully within the traditional structures. The examples chosen here cover a wide range. Some are particularly close to the "alternative schools" model; others are more especially community-based enterprises; yet others are more concerned with job creation than entrepreneurial training as such. They seem to represent points on the long continuum of possibilities linking education to production in enterprises organised for and essentially by young people. As such, they frequently suffer from numerous problems, often due, in the words of one American observer, to the fact that they "combine in one place all the problems of small business with all the problems of high school drop-outs" (private communication, PPV in Philadelphia, 1979). However, they also offer potentially valuable possibilities for young people to learn many skills, to run independent enterprises, to learn to organise, to calculate and weigh up the benefits and the merits of alternative courses of action and to make investments of resources while at the same time being sheltered from the excessively drastic results of their occasional mistakes. For many young people, this apprenticeship is their only possibility of experimentation in such an undertaking and in the skills leading to the potential for them of creating their own jobs rather than waiting to compete for already existing but all-too-scarce labour market operations.

On the end of the spectrum most closely connected to formal education are two American examples. The Alternative Schools Network in Chicago is a coalition of 45 community-based schools that is developing 12 youth-operated projects in five inner-city neighbourhoods. The 12 projects will eventually train 200 young persons to run their own businesses, such as auto maintenance shop and a food co-operative. The schools concerned are formal educational institutions but organised in a non-traditional manner. The aim of the youth projects is principally training but it is also intended to create permanent jobs.

In other United States cities (such as Baltimore, Philadelphia and Seattle) federal funds are being utilised to help young people from disadvantaged areas build their vocational skills at the same time as they work for a high school diploma. The Baltimore programme, for example, has 4 major goals: "to reduce truancy and dropping-out by providing potential drop-outs with part-time work experience on condition they remain at school and maintain good attendance; to encourage drop-outs to return to school, thereby enhancing their future employability; to provide meaningful work experience to disadvantaged teenagers in order to develop positive work attitudes and to ease the transition to full-time employment; and to demonstrate that a program entitling disadvantaged youth to part-time jobs can be administered on a massive scale and still provide a meaningful experience to participants" (United States Department of Labor, 1979).

To meet these goals the Baltimore youth programme has over 1,000 worksites, 360 in the private sector and more than 700 in the private non-profit and public sector, which provide nearly 10,000 young people with education and jobs. Fifteen hundred returning drop-outs are enrolled in 11 alternative education schemes.

Many of these programmes are explicitly linked to the local labour market and emphasize maritime and maritime-related jobs, prevalent in the area. In conjunction with the jobs, the Community College of Baltimore middle college has introduced a special series of classes held in regular college settings. These intensive academic courses prepare at the first level for the high-school equivalency certificate, the General Educational Development Diploma. After completion of this, students can pass into 1- or 2-year associate arts degree courses at the college. In this way the college is helping to pull down the barriers to good local jobs in the maritime sphere and elsewhere for students who lack high school diplomas. At the same time, the young people concerned spend 15 hours a week on minimum wage jobs and thus can not only build their vocational skills but also feel they are participating in the adult world as worthwhile members.

A second American example is one in which a South Bronx community organisation, the Argus Community Inc., affiliated with the New York City Board of Education, reaches 200 young people. It is organising them into Youth Enterprises, each of which has four components: a tutoring service; a publications laboratory (to edit and publish a bilingual community newspaper in the South Bronx); an escort, companion and errand project providing direct and indirect services for the elderly; and a building maintenance project.

This formula is one that is particularly important because, unlike most other such ventures, it ensures that young people in different streams of education co-operate together in a single interest. In the project companies, the tutoring service employs college-bound high school students as elementary school counsellors and tutors who work alongside their peers in practical-oriented courses in the same enterprises.

Our last example here is of potential applicability in most OECD countries. This is the New Haven Constitution, in New Haven, Connecticut. In this scheme young people develop a job location and placement service and administer it for their peers. A remedial programme of instruction in basic skills is operated by the New Haven schools and serves as a bridge between the city's public high schools and the youth-run job programme. In the scheme, young people not only learn about existing and potential job opportunities in their local area by participating in running it, but also gain valuable experience in entrepreneurial activity and management of an enterprise that involves the organisation of data and people rather than the manufacture of a product (Information derived from Youthwork, 1979).

In Australia too, some provision is made to train young people in business management and at the same time provide them with loans and grants to help them start their own businesses. There are schemes in operation in South Australia, for instance, which aim specifically at the 15-18 age-range. The same state also has schemes of business management for the same age group. The take-up rate, however, seems to be disappointingly low and officials administering the scheme feel that schools locally should play a much greater role in fostering the skills and enterprise related to small business and co-operatives (private communication, Department of Industrial Affairs and Employment, Adelaide, 1981).

In Britain, the Manpower Services Commission sponsors a variety of schemes which include businesses run as training ventures for young people. Within the Youth Opportunities Programme (YOP), training workshops make and sell products or provide services. These workshops are part run by, but are not controlled by, the young trainees. Some, however, are extremely successful and could, with changes in the conditions of funding, take off and provide permanent jobs as well as training by becoming established as small businesses or production co-operatives (Jackson, 1980, p. 9).

In Denmark, the Ministry of Education has been involved, since 1978, in co-operation with local and country authorities in subsidising experiments that combine education with production programmes. These schemes involve providing young people with training as well as production opportunities involving the sale of real goods and services. Grants are available for the salaries of teachers and instructors, the purchase of materials and equipment, rent and purchase of premises and equipment, transport and living expenses, including pocket money. The scheme is supervised at national level by an Experiment Committee appointed by the Ministry of Education (Ministry of Education, Ministry of Labour, 1978).

2. From employment to education to employment

So far in this section the emphasis has been on the initial training of young people, both in technical skills so as to improve the quality of labour available in a given area and in the more general, but necessary, skills of entrepreneurship. Recurrent education is, however, also important.

Young people are not the only residents in urban areas of the kind discussed. Their parents and even grand-parents are also often in need of employment. Frequently they need to improve their existing skills or retrain in new ones. Equally often, given the concentrations of unemployment among adults in many areas, they too are going to be involved in job creation schemes which involve entrepreneurship on a community or individual basis. They too can be involved in production co-operatives and to do so they also need to learn new attitudes and capabilities. The many new schemes being set up all require a response from both the formal and informal education systems if they are to make a long-term impact on their areas. All are of interest to policy-makers concerned with a greater link between education and local development.

C. THE COLLEGE AS A COMMUNITY DEVELOPMENT RESOURCE

"Academic institutions have for too long regarded their obligation to society as discharged by the production of graduates. That is, of course, a social service. But in circumstances as socially damaging as those now in prospect in South Wales, they are the strongest reasons why the academic part of the community should find ways of returning a more immediate benefit to the economy in which it is embedded" (Times Educational Supplement, N°. 3325, 1980).

This polemic was provoked by the recent proposed closure of the British Steel Corporation's plant in South Wales. It does, however, suggest a more general need for a closer look at the relationship between institutions of higher and further education - universities, technical institutes, etc. - and the regeneration of their local communities. The areas specifically covered, of course, will vary by the level of institution, university constituencies generally being larger than those of junior colleges. The scale, however, is less important than the effective turning of attention by the institutions concerned towards these constituencies. For a variety of reasons (some of which are described in the paper by Falk to be quoted below) many have been reluctant to do this. Nevertheless, there is now an increasing willingness in many OECD countries for colleges and universities and the public authorities that control them to reconsider their role and to take active steps in the direction of greater involvement in their local communities. A recent OECD project, entitled Higher Education and the Commmunity: New Partnerships and Interaction stressed many of the issues that concern us here. Detailed discussion of them may be found in the final report for that project. A few examples of particular strategies will be cited here.

1. Improvement of the quality of life

Community colleges in the United States usually consider that one of their major concerns is to improve the quality of life in their areas. In the Florida Junior College at Jacksonville, for example, there is an Urban Skills Center, a Center for the Continuing Education of Women, a series of courses in Basic Adult

Education as well as tailor-made, customised workforce training schemes for local employers. The College also participates in University Year for Action programmes which link education and work simultaneously in a variety of fields. It is now involved in developing community supported placements so as to guarantee continuation after the end of special federal funding for many schemes. That it should do this is a measure of the success of such courses and of the benefits that have been apparent for students, college, participating agencies and the community. In such link programmes, students receive the funds necessary to continue their education, the college acquires an opportunity to assist in the training of future workers while also profiting from the presence of low-cost supplementary part-time and full-time staff. Finally, the community receives increased services through additional and better-trained manpower.

Community colleges can be involved in other ways, too. They participate, for instance, in the complete spectrum of particular problem-solving in the community, from needs assessment to analysis of the problem and development of alternative solutions and the provision of the educational component of that solution. In Illinois, for instance, Aurora Community College became involved in dealing with a serious housing problem in its city. Other colleges provide in-service training for local public service employees (San Francisco). Others again have made special efforts to co-ordinate their activities with those of local agencies. In Rochester, a city in New York State, a consortium of business, industry, government and higher education has been established to identify urban problems and indicate where higher education might help. Initiative for its establishment came from the community. Entitled the Urbanarium, the new organisation is "to assist the community in identifying issues facing the greater Rochester area, provide an independent forum for clarifying policy alternatives and to improve institutional capabilities for solving community problems". Acting as a broker for different groups the Urbanarium has conducted many activities including developing information on specific issues and conducting leadership training courses.

In Europe, Sweden appears to have taken the lead in this particular aspect of university initiative. There, one new institution, the University College of Lulea, has been founded with the explicit intention of helping stimulate the surrounding community. The college has built up close relationships with both trade unionists and employers. After initial difficulties in making itself known, it now responds to demands from local groups for specialised training and other resources that may be used for development. It offers R & D for projects that have a direct bearing on the region's development. Although Lulea is not a poor inner-city area, the principles on which its college operates and the methods used are applicable in many places.

2. Business and entrepreneurial training

Some institutions of higher education in France have begun to take initiatives on the one hand linking them more closely to production activities specific to their locality, and on the other to encouraging small and new businesses. France's most prestigious undergraduate school of business management education, the Ecole des Hautes Etudes Commerciales (HEC), for instance, set up in 1973 an association for "research and development of teaching procedures encouraging the creation and development of small, medium and new enterprises". This association, to which 26 commercial schools belonged by 1980, uses publicly provided funds to produce courses for enterprise development which both engineering and commercial schools are then encouraged to use. Since 1972, HEC itself has offered special courses to its own students on creating and developing small businesses (Avenirs, N°. 311, 1980, p. 37).

Such schools are semi-private in France and the wholly public universities have been slower to act. A number of propositions in the latter sector, however, are now on the drawing board. In the region of Provence-Alpes-Côte d'Azur, for instance, a joint committee of elected regional officials, university members and student and teachers' unions has been planning ways in which the university's resources can be exploited, for example in the greater use of the expertise of university teachers by local policy-makers, or by the university providing research, teaching and other facilities for the use of local people in and outside business.

In the domain of community enterprise, the United States have probably achieved most, both by universities and community colleges located in deprived urban areas. Some are directly linked to community enterprises. In New York City, for instance, the Harlem Commonwealth Council is an example of a community development corporation started with major help from two academic institutions, Columbia University and the New School for Social Research. The academic group made basic economic studies of Harlem and showed the feasibility of specific industrial and commercial alternatives for community development. Local community leaders, however, actually build the CDC organisation and its programme (Center for Community Economic Development, 1975). In Roxbury, a once riot-torn poor black community just outside Boston, the Community College has been successfully involved with local housing rehabilitation and improvement groups, providing technical assistance and training. That example is repeated with variations in very many communities throughout the country.

In the private sector, companies already existing often need help, and in individual cases colleges can provide cheap R & D training for management and workers. Small firms generally do little training themselves but are big users of skilled labour which it is too expensive for them to train. This is general to many Member countries. More specifically in the areas concerned in this report, businesses run by minority populations are both especially important and in need of special assistance. The great importance of offering courses in management skills specifically for them has been brought out in a recent report. This points out that all minority-owned businesses together constitute only a tiny percentage of United States enterprises and that their total sales are roughly the equivalent of one large corporation. According to a Dun and Bradstreet study, 90 per cent of all business failures are due to poor management. Minority populations rarely get management experience even in other companies and their need for such education is therefore even greater. They are doubly disadvantaged because they do not learn about business in a managerial or ownership capacity at home, within their families, as do other more fortunate children. Formal training in and early exposure to business possibilities is therefore especially important for them. The same situation is true of many similar populations, whether minority or migrant as well as native, in Europe.

In Britain, an Urbed paper entitled "Linking the College and the Community: fostering new enterprise" (1978) suggested three principal areas of activity. Some relate to new entrepreneurship; others to aid to existing enterprises.

The first is the identification of potential local entrepreneurial populations. For the creation of new enterprises, whether individually-oriented or community-based, the potential clients for specific courses and activities would seem to be:

- redundant executives;

- women insufficiently fulfilled at home;

- business graduates or engineers with advanced degrees who cannot obtain the jobs they feel they merit;

- immigrants, particularly from East Africa or the United States with traditions of hard work and independence and some capital;

- former community workers or teachers who are "fed up with the system";

- individuals who want to prove the value of alternative lifestyles, such as co-operatives, or alternative technology.

These groups are not likely all to be found in any given area but at least some will be and attention needs to be paid to deciding which are the most entrepreneurially promising local populations and recruiting and selecting suitable candidates as well as supporting them in the crucial early days of their new enterprises. Studies of the potential can be made by the college.

The second recommended area of activity concerns the help colleges can give in adapting appropriate technology - both in research and training. The third area is teaching for existing entrepreneurs, especially in the field of management.

3. Links between colleges and development planners

In a number of OECD countries there has been specific recognition by governments that tertiary level education institutions located in urban areas can contribute to the regeneration of neighbourhoods. In Great Britain, under the aegis of Inner-City Partnership Schemes funded by the Department of the Environment, City University and the Polytechnic of North London are joining forces to assess the contribution they can make to the revitalisation of Hackney and Islington. A field officer based in Hackney has been appointed and she has already put small businesses in the area in touch with the relevant university and college departments, notably the management and business schools. "Both institutions see the project as an opportunity to provide valuable experience for students in dealing with real situations as well as benefiting the community" ("Colleges help revive inner city area", Times Higher Education Supplement, N°. 386, 1980).

In the United States, similar arrangements are coming into being. In one, the federal government and seven national higher education institutions have signed an agreement under which urban colleges and universities will co-operate with the Department of Housing and Urban Development (HUD) to help revitalise the cities where they are located. The associations, which represent all sectors of public and private education, will co-sponsor a "center for college and university partners in community development" which will give technical assistance to educational institutions planning to undertake urban improvement projects in co-operation with city governments. Not only will educational and cultural programmes specifically aimed at the poor black minority and unemployed be provided, but courses will be developed to provide technical skills for city governments to improve planning, management and the delivery of public services ("Deal to boost urban development is signed", Times Higher Education Supplement", N°. 386, 1980).

4. Reaching the disadvantaged

In Canada some community colleges have been seeking new ways of reaching the more disadvantaged of their potential constituents. Doing so involves the colleges taking considerable trouble to identify local needs. The Saskatchewan Community Colleges have been particularly active in reaching out to the members of local communities especially in need but also especially unlikely to seek education of their own volition. The College of Saskatoon, for example, conducts courses for community development, individual skill improvement and basic literacy for disadvantaged groups - particularly for women.

The approaches here are important. The Saskatoon College identifies local needs by various mass media approaches to the general public and the seeking of continual feedback. It advertises that the College responds to public requests, it asks part-time learners for their follow-up requests and keeps close contact with the library, the city council and other established groups, as well as using the more usual publicity techniques. Recognising, however, that these methods do not reach the lower end of the economic scale, the College also maintains an office in a disadvantaged area where programmers work with smaller groups and agencies to ensure that appropriate courses are provided. Concentration is on all residents of one area, on women and on native populations living in the city. Most of the courses are new. Many are non-credit and are put on jointly with the local School Board. Others provide high school upgrading. Methods are varied and imaginatively designed to cope with the special needs of the populations served. They include one-week camps for single mothers and their children and a Learning Resource Centre for basic literacy where the people drop in as often as they please rather than follow a course. The College makes a special effort to recruit and train as teachers members of the disadvantaged communities themselves, believing that people "who have been there" make for more effective learning in this context. Courses are planned, too, in consultation with the learners so as to ensure immediate relevance to needs (Pepper, 1978).

Colleges and universities, then, can play a greater role in a variety of efforts to improve the situation of people living in disadvantaged city areas and through them to improve the area. Some of these involve the development of broad skills and the capacity to take action in community self-help and the provision of services. Others are aimed more at improving the locality's productive base.

At this point, it is appropriate to reproduce a paper contributed to the Venice Conference by Nicholas Falk, Director of Urbed (an urban research and economic development unit operating in London), for it deals specifically with innovations, actual and desirable, in the role colleges can play in encouraging local economic enterprise. Since it was written, more schemes have been reported upon and notes on these have been incorporated in his text.

D. LINKING THE COLLEGE WITH LOCAL ENTERPRISE
(contributed by Nicholas Falk)

How far can colleges help to reverse the vicious circle of decline from which many urban areas suffer? Over the past 3 years URBED (Urban and Economic Development) Ltd., a non-profit organisation, through its research and consultancy activities has examined initiatives that colleges have taken in Britain and abroad. This has formed part of a larger research programme concerned with ideas and solutions to the problems of local economic development. The data presented here largely refer to Great Britain but the general ideas are applicable elsewhere.

The problems of economic decline are putting pressure on resources, and education is particularly vulnerable to cuts. Yet our research, in summary, leads to the conclusion that the interests of colleges and the community in promoting local economic development should overlap. There are many precedents for how colleges can take the initiative, but these are unlikely to achieve their full potential unless they are part of a planned effort. The problem is that there are many obstacles to collaboration both on the part of the college and local businesses. Hence we argue for a series of measures whereby government, particularly through local authorities, can be used to the full. In what follows, we deal in turn with:

1) the problem of local economic development

2) college initiatives

3) the obstacles of collaboration

4) the public policy implications.

1. The problem of local economic development

The economic recession is leading to public expenditure cuts, and education is particularly vulnerable. Education has come under attack for failing to produce the kind of people employers want, both at secondary school and at higher or college levels. School leavers have been seeking jobs rather than risk unemployment at the end of a college education. Cuts in student grants and capital expenditure threaten expansion plans, and are causing some colleges to reduce the courses they offer. Much research is popularly considered to be irrelevant. As the cuts are intended to shift resources into the expansion of the "productive" and private sectors, it is important to know how far the activities of colleges, tertiary education institutions and universities are and can be relevant to the problems of local economic development in large cities. The basic problems to be faced are those of economic decline, physical decay and social stress.

a) Economic decline

All the major British cities have suffered from and are still bearing the costs of a permanent change in their employment structure. Many cities, especially in the inner areas, have lost the traditional sources of highly paid manual jobs, in manufacturing and basic large scale industries like steel, gas, the railways and docks. Though they have gained new jobs, these have tended to be office jobs. At the lower levels, they have largely been filled by women returning to work and at the higher ones by people who live a long way from the inner city. In neither case has the situation done much to improve local skills or provide stable, skilled and well-paid jobs for local people. Furthermore, many of the sectors that recently provided extra jobs are unlikely to continue to grow; either they are affected by public expenditure constraints (like education and health) or by technological change and relocation away from cities (like insurance and banking).

As a consequence, small firms in these areas have assumed much greater importance as a potential source of jobs for those who would otherwise be unemployed. Before unemployment began to rise rapidly, little effort had been made in Britain to encourage the growth of small businesses compared with countries such as the United States. It was assumed that their decline was inevitable. Now there is a growing public realisation that few large firms will be attracted back to the inner city and equally that the public sector is not likely to expand to fill the gap. Hence attention has shifted to finding ways of encouraging more small firms to start and grow. Research findings show that in the United States, firms with fewer than 20 employees account for some 60 per cent of the new jobs created between 1969 and 1976. This analysis has reinforced public belief that small enterprise can be important in the solution of Britain's persistent economic problems.

Ways of making this solution effective, however, are harder to find. Acting on decisions made by entrepreneurs is a highly complex undertaking. The problems faced by existing firms and potential entrepreneurs are multiple and require varied solutions. Moreover, whereas small firms in general face problems because they lack resources and the ability to influence their environment, small firms in inner city areas face even greater difficulties. For example, our experience, backed up by other research studies, indicates that the capabilities and interests of the management of the small firms prevalent in inner areas are rarely adequate to adapt to fundamental change. These enterprises are often run by old, and poorly educated owners who blame their difficulties (with some justification) on other people. The businesses are fragmented and often fighting for a share of declining markets, in the face of cheaper imports and the concentration of buying power in fewer hands. Secondly, there are all too few new firms, and the kinds of manufacturing businesses that might grow large are often set up by people who live in smaller towns and villages away from urban conurbations. In the inner city areas, too, even those firms that could in principle expand often in practice cannot do so because of difficulties with obtaining suitable premises, adequate labour, or development finance. Finally, even where resources may be available, the sheer size of a city makes it hard to obtain appropriate advice and information. Hence unemployment rises in the face of the paradoxical situation that many goods and services are still hard to obtain and small firms complain they cannot secure staff. The problem therefore on the one hand is the encouragement of existing businesses, which may involve them in quite considerable changes but also on the other of the creation of new ones.

b) <u>Physical decay and social stress</u>

A combination of economic decline and physical decay creates the conditions in which social tensions flourish. One manifestation of such tensions is particularly unfortunate for the realisation of local developmental potential. The college, or the local university, instead of being seen as a source of help, is often distrusted. It seems often to be regarded as the property of the privileged few, supported at public expense, studying or researching irrelevant subjects. Hostility between "town and gown" is common. A poor, drab and insecure environment is unattractive to live in and few staff reside close to the college. Though the colleges are fixed by their buildings, the connections with the surrounding area may lessen as an area deteriorates. This is a great pity. The interests of college and community do not have to conflict and indeed changes in technology as the motor for industrial development may make them coincide. Economic development is becoming increasingly less dependent on human muscle power but more dependent on brain power.

In other words, economic development is now bound up with the ability to apply knowledge to the design, manufacture and distribution of products and services. Information is now a resource like energy or capital equipment. Consequently, colleges are playing an even more vital role than before. This has been recognised in a number of countries.

2. Existing college initiatives

Many colleges and universities are seizing their opportunities. Many individuals within them have seen the need to build better links with local industry, and there is now a promising range of experiments throughout Britain. They are developing a range of ways in which the special resources of colleges and universities - people, facilities and purchasing power - can be used to further local economic development.

The "centres of knowledge" - polytechnics, colleges and universities and teaching hospitals - occupy large areas of land in the inner areas of our cities, and are major sources of economic activity in their own right. They are a source of ideas and information. They are also absorbers of information and can use the learning resources of the local community just as the community can learn from the college. The raw material of the education process - its sources - are the people and things, and the institutions that embrace them in the "world out there".

Knowledge is knowledge about something - for example, atomic particles, social groups or bureaucratic structures. Know-how is acquired in relation to something or someone. That something or someone can be chosen from among relevant local situations and problems and relevant local people and groups. Thus, the educational sources of an area are as much its economy, buildings and residents, as its resources are the colleges and centres of knowledge. The interaction is important and ways need to be found of developing it.

The various possible ways of drawing on a college's resources are analysed below in relation to the main functions a college performs. First there is the function of teaching, or passing on knowledge. Second comes research, or generating knowledge. Finally, there is what we have called service, or utilising a college's resources for the community's benefit.

a) Teaching

There are many ways in which teaching can be more especially beneficial to local enterprise. These vary from making greater efforts to attract local students to incorporating local factors into the curricula of the courses taught. Doing this may involve the college in gathering more systematic information on its local economy and taking the lead in identifying areas of local need which could be matched to local skills as developed through courses at the college. Four fields of activity in particular should be recognised as of potential value in this general context.

Tailor-made courses. Many technical colleges or polytechnics, and sometimes universities, offer technical and business courses that serve large companies in their locality. Often these are tailor-made to fit the individual client's needs. The college's orientation at present is often towards a particular enterprise but the ideas of tailor-made courses could be enlarged to fit the needs of a wider section of the community.

Student projects. One important way of gathering information on the local area and increasing the awareness of students about its problems and potentialities may be tried. This involves augmenting the number of student projects which focus on local matters and areas of concern. Some courses are particularly suitable for such initiatives, notably perhaps the General Education in Engineering programme on the science side particularly, but also in the human services sector; such courses may bring to light not only new information but also be used to develop new ways of solving concrete problems.

The Teaching Company scheme. Teaching Companies are important new initiatives, formalised recently, following the parliamentary investigation into university-industry relations. The scheme began in 1975 and is jointly funded by the Department of Industry and the Science Research Council. It aims to encourage well-qualified first degree students in engineering or physical science to develop production engineering skills (to MSc/PhD standard) by working in a company for a 2-3 year period, while also improving the productive efficiency of the company. The concept is very similar to that of the teaching hospital, since the trainees are company-based, with an academic supervisor from college who can arrange trainee tutoring. Schemes are now operating at more than seven colleges and universities. By late February 1981 this number had risen to 26 with many more in the pipeline. This rapid increase attests to the success of the idea in the eyes of both academics and businessmen. Two are now operating in Ulster, from Ulster Polytechnic, of which one is run in conjunction with the Northern Ireland Development Agency.

Small business units. Courses particularly designed for small enterprises within a college's neighbourhood are unfortunately still comparatively rare and small business units like those at London and Manchester Business Schools have a national rather than local student catchment and focus. However, some thirty-one colleges in the United Kingdom are now offering courses in small business management and it may well be possible to increase the <u>local</u> content of the courses. These courses are aimed at people already running small companies. It would be extremely useful however to develop courses for people thinking of creating their own enterprises. There are only a few courses for new entrepreneurs. These are now running at Manchester, Durham, City of London Business Schools, plus Teesside and St. Helen's Polytechnics, the Anglian Regional Management Centre and a few others but need greater localisation in poorer areas. One college-based initiative in its locality is being held at Sheffield, which has also run courses to help ICI executives start new firms.

There are also many other ways in which colleges may assist small companies. For example, in the United States close links between colleges and local industry are made through such activities as the use of business school students as consultants to small business. The scheme run by the Small Business Institutes, and financed by the government's Small Business Administration, is regarded as one of the most successful ways of helping small enterprises. Faculty members too are often involved as consultants or even directors of local firms. In other cases, such as Stanford University, science parks have been developed to encourage local industry to grow as a means of providing extra income for university staff and better local employment prospects for their graduates. At Stanford this initiative forms an essential part of Silicon Valley and a model that has been copied in 120 places in North America.

In Europe, both France and Italy are following the United States model. Universities are to be the catalysts around which new towns develop. There is also a major science park being developed in the South of France in an area of some 8,000 acres. Southern Italy too is apparently hoping to use universities as part of its regional policy for attracting industry to its depressed areas. In Germany the links between universities and industry have long been close. In less developed countries too, universities often play a crucial role in local economic development programmes, particularly where small business is concerned. Like the church in earlier centuries, colleges as centres of knowledge could increasingly be the focal point of community development.

b) <u>Research</u>

There is much colleges and universities can do in the research field too. Indeed, that field may be theirs <u>par excellence</u>. A wide range of applied technological research is undertaken by individual academics, especially within universities. In Britain there are also three significant national approaches to the problem. These are the University-Industry committee, Centres of Expertise and Research Parks.

<u>University-industry committees</u>: Most universities and polytechnics will have some form of research and consultancy committee. These tend to be very loosely run and seldom aim to co-ordinate more than a proportion of research activity, but in some universities, such as Oxford, a committee exists with a full-time Executive Secretary and backing from industry as well as the Science Research Council to co-ordinate university research with the needs of industry.

<u>Centres of Expertise</u>: Individuals or departments within a university may develop special expertise which can form the basis for specialist units aimed at promoting use of this expertise by industry. Such units are typically funded for a 3-year initial period by the Wolfson Foundation, or University Grants Committee, but are expected to become self-supporting from income after this time. They become a two-way channel for passing ideas out of the college and for attracting research contracts into the college. The Institute of Offshore Engineering at Heriot-Watt University in Edinburgh is a classic example of such a unit's development.

<u>Research and Science Parks</u>: A Research Park is a particular type of industrial estate where new firms, or laboratories of existing firms, set up specifically to conduct technological development. There are a great number of these in the United States, associated in some way with particular universities. In America, these Parks contain a mixture of pure research units and new technology-based manufacturing enterprises. A good example of a pure research park in the United Kingdom is again at Heriot-Watt.

The importance of this idea can be seen by its adoption in other countries. In Adelaide, South Australia, a new high technology park is to be established on land adjacent to the campus of the South Australian Institute of Technology. It will be controlled jointly by representatives of industry, academic institutions and the government. It will encourage closer working relationships between researchers and manufacturers. Not only is the Park expected to strengthen the local industry and employment base but also, in the words of the South Australian Minister for Industrial Affairs, to have a "tremendous impact" on the academic standard and reputation of the South Australian Institute of Technology (reported in the <u>Canberra Times</u>, 1981). (Ed.).

<u>Industrial Research Groups</u>: These groups bring together technological, design and possibly business expertise, and make them available to enterprises or other local organisations. A group can be set up as a formal company as, for instance, at Queen Mary College in East London where an Industrial Research Company has been formed to exploit the university's distinctive competence in a number of areas. In each, one division of the company markets the inventions made within the college. The markets are largely other research and technological establishments but it may be possible to extend such activities so that they focus on the needs of and benefit other local institutions or enterprises.

In such cases the research does not have to deal only with traditional or well-established production methods. Indeed, they may have a special contribution to make in innovations which are of particular benefit to local economic activity and with encouraging experimentation. At North East London Polytechnic, for example, the <u>Centre for Alternative Industrial and Technological Systems</u> (CAITS) is concerned with devising and testing out new technology at an intermediate level, or one that is more appropriate to worker demands and which could help to create new jobs in areas threatened with job closure. Originally set up to meet the needs of Lucas Aerospace, they are now also very concerned with helping new co-operatives to develop in East London.

Research Parks are similar to Science Parks, which are a kind of specialised industrial estate which provides a high quality environment for:

- pure research firms which may be part of a large diverse company, perhaps multi-national, or which may be independent self-supporting small or medium-sized firms;

- manufacturing firms which are based on new or recent developments in science or technology, such as firms in laser technology or micro-electronics.

This concept has been most widely developed in the United States and Canada, where there are over 82 science parks, employing over 140,000 people. The idea is being copied in France, where colleges are being utilised as the catalyst for New Town development, in Southern Italy, where the aim is to copy the American model as a means of reviving a poor region, and in the United Kingdom.

The examples in Britain which are linked to universities are both on a much smaller scale than the average American model, and hence cannot offer the synergy that comes where there are a large number of different firms in related businesses in an area. There is thus as yet nothing in Britain to compare with the Stanford Industrial Park, where the drive came from the Dean of Engineering. His vision was to build up the academic and financial strength of the university by attracting first-class faculty through the provision of consulting opportunities. They would then produce good students, who would work locally. Some would make fortunes which they would give to help Stanford University. The original aim was not local development as such but there seems little doubt that the Industrial Park is a major factor in the local prosperity of the area.

Since this was written, the University of Edinburgh has developed a series of entrepreneurial activities in microelectronics. The research and development work of the university has encouraged many companies in the field to locate or relocate in the Lothian region around the city. The education facilities in microelectronics offered are becoming a factor in the decisions made by firms originally brought by the Scottish

Development Agency. The Science Research Council has encouraged the activities in the university by investing money in M.Sc. courses to train the necessary specialised manpower for the microelectronics industry and research money has followed too.

Another alternative model is provided by the Regional Adaptive Technology Centre concept, which has been tried out in Hawaii and Ghana, among other places. The aim is to develop products that meet local capabilities, both upgrading existing firms and fostering new firms. While there is no direct equivalent in the United Kindom, an embryonic example is the link between Fife Job Creation Workshops and Duncan of Jordanstone School of Art, where local colleges have been asked to design products that meet the criteria of developing profitable products that are labour-intensive and appropriate to the skills available, and that yield satisfying work. Another model is the Centre for Industrial Innovation at the University of Strathclyde.

c) Service

The dividing line between applied research and "service" is thin. Service can range from the provision of technical and business information through the development of processes and products to the actual marketing of innovations. Some more interesting examples at present in operation are the following.

Technical Information Services. These exist at four colleges and also at some public libraries (e.g. Lambeth), with the aim of providing easy access to information for local companies that do not have library systems.

Industrial Liaison Officers. At the heart of the college's relationship with local industry for some time were the Industrial Liaison Bureaux. The Bureaux used experienced industrialists based at over 60 colleges (one or two staff) to provide a free visiting service to small firms (less than 500 employees) in the local area. Each had an Industrial Liaison Officer (ILO) who used his experience to define small firms' problems and to recommend appropriate sources of help where he was not able to advise himself.

ILO functions have been reduced for financial reasons but now include:

- facilitating industry's access to college facilities (e.g. testing facilities, special equipment, consultancy by staff, etc.);

- advertising and/or selling college courses to industry;

- acting as information service to industry and referral to sources of advice;

- aiding students' employment during sandwich courses.

Low-Cost Automation Centres (LCAs). Low-cost automation consists in the use of pneumatic, hydraulic and electronic techniques to improve productivity in industry. Centres such as the one at Sunderland Polytechnic employ 1-4 industrially experienced staff, are based in college largely self-supporting from income. Functions can now include:

- advice on choice of automation equipment (free service, subsidised by grants from the Department of Industry);

- consultancy on automation design, manufacture and prototypes;

- practical courses for industry on automation techniques.

Departmental Consultancies. Individuals in college departments sometimes combine to form a consultancy unit which they staff on a part-time basis to fit in with education and research activities. Such units aim to provide consultancy services to enterprises and to give staff an opportunity to gain practical experience. Students gain indirectly from the feedback of the staff experiences and their incorporation into lectures.

Consultancy "Companies". Companies have been established by ten universities to provide services to industry. They typically employ 15-20 industrially experienced full-time staff. Functions vary across the companies but they include:

- consultancy work for enterprises in various fields of expertise, including developing new products;

- commercial development of college innovations and possible manufacture;

- performing an Industrial Liaison function for college.

Innovation Centres. The Innovation Centre was originally an American creation. Three experimental centres now exist at M.I.T., Carnegie-Mellon and Oregon Universities and others are planned. The Centres are associated with engineering courses, but a wide range of enterprises and products have spun-off as a result. At M.I.T. the focus is on invention, at Carnegie on innovation and at Oregon on diffusion and evaluation. In Scotland, a form of Innovation Centre has been developed over the past few years at Strathclyde University and it is hoped that others may be created.

New Enterprise Workshop. After creating and licensing out know-how to existing businesses, it may make sense for some colleges to go on to the next stage, that of developing working prototypes. This requires equipment and premises, which may be owned by the college, or provided by another agency. Four distinct models can be identified. The first is where the college provides simply the expertise. This applies to, for example, Paisley College in Scotland, where the regional authority provides the premises, and where the workshop facilities are made available to budding entrepreneurs who can obtain back-up support from the college. Similar ideas have also been tried out elsewhere, including Northern Ireland by the Local Enterprise Development Unit, though without such a close college involvement.

A second model involves the college in providing the premises, as in the case of Enterprise Lancaster, where a former furniture factory that provided the first home of Lancaster University has been divided into small units. These are administered now by the City and cater for new technologically based firms. In a third variant, the college also provides equipment and staff expertise too, as at Aston University. Though the formal examples may be rare, there are no doubt many wily entrepreneurs who use college facilities when they are starting up.

Finally, colleges can also become directly involved with creating new employment locally. This may be done either on their own premises, as in the case of Newcastle Polytechnic, or in association with independent workshops, as in the example Duncan of Jordanston College of Art's involvement with Fife Enterprises quoted above.

3. <u>Improving the links between college and community: Four policy suggestions</u>

Analysis suggests that the divide between colleges and industry that frequently exists at the local level is too fundamental to be closed simply through exhortation. Yet the experiments we have examined in Britain and abroad convince us that the public benefits from linking colleges more closely with their local communities could be considerable in the long term. We recommend the following four measures to promote better links:

a) <u>Use of social audits</u>

Just as the performance of private companies is monitored through financial audits which help to focus management attention on improving profits, so the performance of public organisations like polytechnics can be influenced by social audits. Instead of relating revenue to student numbers and staff income to teaching time, consideration should be explicitly given to the college's contribution to the development of the local community in all its aspects, economic, social and cultural.

The social audit is a means of identifying resources and planning how to use them, as well as a method of assessing performance. Rather than doing a comprehensive inventory of everything that is going on, it is better to focus on a few areas where change is possible. The relevant questions to be answered include:

i) What do the staff and students of the college think of their institution as a whole (or sections of it)? How do they assess its:

- purposes
- particular functions
- relevant communities?

ii) What unusual resources does the college have (or sections of it)? How do these relate to:

- institutional inputs:

    . people
    . facilities
    . purchasing power

- educational outputs:

    . research
    . teaching
    . service?

iii) What are the most significant communities of concern to the college? Are they:

- present sponsoring bodies:

    . local
    . regional
    . national
    . international

- potential "clients" within the community:

    . educational
    . working
    . residential?

iv) How far are local sources being tapped in the educational process? What use is made of them in:

- lectures and case studies
- projects
- sandwich programmes
- teaching companies
- etc.?

v) How far are college resources being fully used in the economic development process? What do they do in relation to:

- giving birth to new enterprises
- helping existing firms survive and grow
- attracting major companies to locate in the area.

The audit is a means of assessing relevance. It could be initiated by the local authority, perhaps in connection with the development of corporate plans or by an individual within the college. However, to succeed it must be a collective effort with the maximum participation of all the staff, rather than a technical exercise to be left to planning or community liaison officers. It needs also to be linked with the production of the regular prospectus and budgeting, so that it is seen as an essential part of the college's function and not as an extra chore.

b) <u>Preparation of local economic development plans</u>

While the social audit is an effective method for finding out what is being done, it can only be a partial guide to what should be done. Most local authorities now have well-established procedures for drawing up corporate or community plans, and these can provide good guides to the problems of the area and to the relevant local authority programmes. They are, however, often weak when it comes to economic development. There are two reasons for this. First, local authority planners are not used to identifying economic opportunities. Second, their powers to influence economic development are limited. Colleges could make a major contribution to the analysis through their economics and business facilities and the plans and analysis would in return provide a wealth of research opportunities for students. In the process it would be far easier than it is now to consider joint projects such as new training programmes. Hence we believe that staff from local colleges should be involved both in drawing up general plans for local economic development and also in examining the particular problems of major local industries.

c) <u>Participation in local enterprise trusts</u>

In many parts of Britain, new initiatives are now being taken to stimulate small businesses. But after the conferences and reports have been digested, the question arises of action to take about the difficulties identified. Often all that is needed is the chance of talking over a problem with an objective outsider, but there is often no one whom the businessman feels he can trust and, indeed, he may well not be able to afford consultancy help.

There are several ways in which the problem can be solved. Some local authorities, like the Greater London Council, have established large departments with industrial advisors. Another solution offered is the network of 12 Small Business Information Centres run by the Department of Industry's Small Business

Division, and a growing band of councillors, who are experienced businessmen. Both these approaches, however, suffer from being associated with government and therefore are not readily trusted. A better approach, we believe, is to set up independent bodies, which have been given the generic name "local enterprise trusts", with the aim of providing a supportive environment. Colleges can then play a crucial role in providing specialised expertise. To date perhaps the most ambitious existing example is the role played by the Durham University Business School in relation to Enterprise North, an association which helps new businessmen throughout the Northern Region. The American model of the Small Business Institutes is worth copying more widely.

The wealth of college resources to be tapped justifies the appointment or re-appointment of Industry Liaison Officers. Such an officer should bring together the various aspects of a college's relationship with the local community and so needs to be a fairly senior appointment. Local enterprise trusts, Chambers of Commerce and other bodies will provide introduction to networks of influence outside the college. Inside the college liaison needs to be made with student groups, careers and housing officers, and with those concerned with running short courses and conferences. To ensure a local focus, it would be best if these organisations were funded by local government as part of their economic development programmes. The London Boroughs of Hackney and Islington are testing out this approach with City University and North London Polytechnic.

d) Creation of new enterprise workshops

One of the most basic needs of new firms is somewhere to work and the provision of a suitable environment is therefore often an effective way of encouraging the birth of new firms. Colleges can contribute to this by providing space either in a spare building or else on land they own for future expansion. Such a development can serve educational purposes, while the income should provide a further incentive to the college. Where their own space is not available, colleges should still develop links with particular buildings or industrial estates that cater for new and technologically-based enterprise.

Several types of "new enterprise workshops" are possible. They range from the "community workshop" which may be run by an adult educational institute, to an innovation centre or even a Science Park, linked to a major university. There is no standard pattern, for if such a scheme is to work it must be tailored to the particular opportunities of the local economy and to the interests and resources of the colleges in the locality.

The funding for such development may come from several sources. As well as providing some spare land or buildings, a college might offer support from the appropriate departments, who would be invited to see the "new enterprise workshop" as an outlet for various of their activities. Consultancies and directorships in new enterprises would be encouraged, particularly where the experience could feed back into the educational sphere. The local authority would orchestrate the development.

* * * * * * * * *

These innovations involve all the actors in the situation in making significant changes. Those changes, hard to initiate, themselves have an educational output. At the same time as they learn specific new ways of doing things, and to take advantage of new opportunities, all those concerned are also learning more generally. They learn more about the workings of their local environment, more about its relationship to national policies and problems, more about the processes of change themselves and the recognition that things can be altered, that individual initiatives count, that the actions of each affect the chances and possibilities of all. In this way perhaps, not only can local economic possibilities be improved but a new sense of community engendered, reducing the isolation felt by so many in poor and depressed city areas and in that way too immeasurably improving their conditions of life.

Part Four

CONCLUSIONS. NOT EDUCATION OR DEVELOPMENT – EDUCATION FOR DEVELOPMENT

Bringing together the data gathered in the course of the ELD Project - as we have attempted to do above - has revealed many of the issues involved in making education more responsive to development goals in urban localities. Above all, perhaps, we may conclude from the experience of many countries and over the last decade that the appropriate policy choice is not education or or development. It is of necessity education for development.

It is also clear that the choice must be education with development. Education alone, even specifically oriented towards development, cannot produce the necessary changes. Just as more generally education cannot solve youth unemployment problems because there are simply not enough jobs, so even education for development cannot of itself make sufficiently substantial differences to the conditions of life prevalent in poor urban neighbourhoods. Our survey shows, however, that there is an increasing recognition of the important part education, both formal and non-formal, has to play in local development and that this could and should be strengthened.

At the same time the survey disclosed where there is particular room for improvement in innovative activity. Most notable here are the content of education and teaching and learning methods - some for specific populations who need special attention, some with issues of finance and administration. Perhaps the most significant advances, however, will be concerned with the specific contribution that education for development can make to solving that most widespread and personally and social destructive problem: long-term youth unemployment.

Education for development

We have seen that development strategies proceed in a number of stages. Development even as a concept is not unitary and in practice means action on a number of fronts. Sustaining improvement policies and programmes and helping them to build up a cumulative effect involves building a critical mass of changes in both concrete conditions and in the attitudes and expectations of local populations. In other words, it involves using and increasing the potential of people as well as material resources.

In view of this diversity, there is no one clearly marked set of prescriptions which can be labelled "education for development". Each of many policies addresses one aspect of the question. Each equally addresses non-development aspects of the individual and the society. However, in the light of the multinational input into the ELD Project, one can discern a series of steps in the general process of development where education can effectively intervene. Taking seriously the new policy orientations towards effective strategies being built up from the community (although using nationally generated resources where necessary) will involve the active participation of local residents at each one of these steps or stages.

Schematically, the approach suggested necessitates:

- increasing information about and making an analysis of the particularities of local problems and their relationship to national trends and issues;

- a sensitisation of the public of local residents to the situation of the area as a whole, rather than just their individual experience of the different aspects;

- devising a plan of action, or rather a series of plans of action, some simultaneous, some serial;

- mustering the necessary resources;

- carrying through the different elements of the projects decided upon;

- evaluating the effects of the activity(ies);

- devising suitable follow-up and links with related projects and groups working in the field.

To this may be added:

- disseminating information about the workings of and the successes and failures of particular development activities to other people and communities who find themselves in similar situations and feed back to policy instigators from the community concerned.

Ideally, of course, the resulting programmes and procedures should lead to a situation where progress in any given domain is "self-generated"; where jobs that last have been created, where good health practices in one field lead to wider health improvements, where housing can be maintained in good condition; where the success of a food co-operative leads to other areas of consumption or production co-operation; where individuals and the community as a whole gain greater self-confidence and greater self-respect. It is ultimately to the creation of this self-generating progress that education must contribute.

At each stage of this process education has both a direct and an indirect role to play. The innovations described in earlier sections show how formal education in schools and colleges can:

- contribute to the collection and dissemination of background information;

- collect and disseminate information on the causes and dimensions of particular problems and possible solutions;

- help young people and adults to contribute individually and in groups to assessing local resources and devising appropriate plans for problem-solving;

- assist with the production of the skills which are necessary for presenting projects, getting them accepted by the appropriate bodies and funded as necessary;

- help pupils and students work directly on the implementation of proposals;

- concentrate technical and organisational skills necessary to the implementation of a whole spectrum of development activities, from private business production and management to public welfare facilities;

- encourage the growth of a sense of community in what are frequently areas of great anomie and personal or familial isolation;

- vastly improve the sense of self-value of local community residents, both through increasing their technical skills and, through showing them through practice that they do count, that they have a contribution to make to publicly valued activities.

Making the role of formal education effective in these spheres involves a reconsideration of many of the traditionally accepted aims and objectives of the educational system. It also has implications for what is taught, how it is taught, how learning is organised, and who should do the teaching. It further raises questions about the location where the teaching and learning should take place, the timing of the process in the life of individuals and the relationship between different forms of learning. It calls into question teacher training, the organisation of educational institutions and the financing of experimental and innovatory strategies. It brings to the fore questions of inter-agency co-operation and the relationship desirable between public and private initiatives and responsibilities. Most important perhaps it brings back onto the public agenda in a particularly salient manner fundamental questions about social justice and equity and ultimately the legitimation of the social order.

All of these issues deserve attention. Some are of greater magnitude and complexity than others. In the context of the present report, two aspects of education need particular mention: curriculum and the reorganisation of the teaching-learning process. In the field of development, school and extra-school development activities, again two aspects are salient: the need for public-private co-operation and the means of organising for successful intervention.

A. EDUCATION-DEVELOPMENT: FORGING AN EFFECTIVE ALLIANCE

1. Curriculum

The word curriculum is used here to cover the totality of learning experiences offered to young people, not just the content of the courses. This designation is of particular significance when, as in education oriented to development, the aim is to promote both understanding and action. Attention must be directed particularly at:

a) widening the what of what is taught to include far greater understanding of, on the one hand, local matters (history and geography, issues and organisations, labour markets and their needs) and, on the other hand, the placing of the local in the national context;

b) inculcating and emphasizing the importance of new attitudes and abilities through education for capacity, which has also been called carrefour education. This involves the development of: organisational skills, mobilisation skills, co-operative skills, communication skills;

c) more specifically, the technical and quasi-technical skills associated with entrepreneurship.

Such a re-orientation of the curriculum will need to be supplemented by the inculcation of technical skills particularly appropriate for local labour markets, including the production and consumption sectors. Then, in their turn, these particular skills will need to be supplemented by the development of new values and attitudes. This is because the socialisation process of much of past educational practice has been antithetical to the imparting of any but academic and specific individual vocational abilities and skills. It has been antithetical to group working, to the development of the ability to weigh up rationally alternative investments of time and resources, and to young people in direct involvement in the production of real goods and services.

Such a separation of young people during school years from the rest of the community, and their segregation in "in-school" activities, has in effect cut them off from positive and maturity-producing experiences. In the deprived areas this has too often meant sentencing young people to spend their days in activities in which they usually perceive themselves as failures, and which, to protect themselves, they at least profess to attach no value.

These attitudes inherent in the traditional curriculum are not positive. They do not indicate to those concerned desirable and achieveable ways of using energy. They do not indicate acceptable paths towards taking responsibility for themselves and others. These are the values and attitudes that must be changed.

2. Teaching methods and the ordering of the learning process

Much education has not been geared to the needs of students in deprived areas. It is time to recognise that much of what has been taught has not even been absorbed. This is because present instructional methods and course contents fail to recognise that:

"over the years of compulsory schooling most students remain concrete thinkers. They require experience and activity as well as verbal transmission to make ideas understandable. They move from the particular to the general and outwards from their own experience ... if we are concerned that students should be turned on by the power of ideas to illumine and extend experience, we should teach ideas and strategies in relation to actual application significant for students in the world they inhabit." (Schools Commission, 1980.)

The lack of success of traditional methods of teaching in many big city schools thus suggests the need for changes both in curriculum focus and in teaching methods. Experiential learning, learning-by-doing, action-learning, even on-the-job training. These are the methods that seem increasingly the most appropriate. The absorption of information by doing involves:

- placing the activity in a relevant context. There is evidence that literacy and numeracy skills can easily be taught successfully where their usefulness is implicit in the activity;

- finding possibilities of producing objects or services that are of real value at the same time as they are graded to students' maturity;

- working in groups rather than individually in a co-operative endeavour;

- de-emphasizing the usual school practice of age-based hierarchy that younger and older can work together;

- breaking down invidious distinctions of the value of "intellectual" and "manual" activities - new definitions of work need to be institutionalised in the schools;

- reallocating timetables so as to allow for learning in non-school agencies and organisations;

- experimenting with various methods of active learning, to include students in role-playing to enable them both to learn the different sides of any real life situation but also to appreciate the opportunities and constraints linked to the occupation of different social and economic positions;

- finding other than lecture methods for teachers, adults, for instance, through the case method.

The importance of this approach can be seen by the success of such strategies as training workshops. In the United Kingdom, for instance, training workshops are regarded as the success story of the job creation programme, not only because they integrate education and work but because:

"They provide real jobs, making and doing worthwhile things in a genuinely productive work setting, with all the status and self-respect that that brings to youngsters who may have been labelled as 'failures' at school ... They are small in size and provide a real community with personal relationship support ... They enable young people of different ages to work and learn together as equals, the younger learning from the maturity of the older." (Youthaid, 1978.)

These workshops are organised for out-of-school youth; they could be introduced into many big city high schools, both "generally" oriented and vocational.

3. Staffing courses

Teaching children and young people in poor metropolitan areas is not easy. These youngsters are almost by definition people who have rejected education. The little ones play truant or are disruptive. The older ones wait only to leave school. Those who have left and later wish to return to education have lost what few good learning habits they had ever acquired.

Teaching in these areas, therefore, requires both special skills and special attitudes. It involves:

- changing the basis of the relationship between teacher and learner;

- the recognition that teaching children and teaching adolescents out of school or adults who are unemployed and educationally and socially deprived demands different and equally specific skills (it has been found, for instance, that teacher-training school students are uncomfortable with adults while university teachers do not have any idea about teaching deprived 16-year-olds);

- training specifically for active involvement in community affairs; this involves activities ranging from training directors of school-based community involvement programmes to inculcating the recognition that teachers are resources of expertise for community use;

- readiness to accept changes in the ordering of the teaching and learning year where appropriate (as, for example, where school-based enterprises require short holidays and longer days);

- preparedness for teachers on occasion to state values and move out from their neutral position;

- readiness where necessary to take the learning to the students rather than wait for them to come to school or college. Adults in particular in poor areas will not go far afield for education, and many groups, such as immigrant women, can only be reached in non-traditional ways and places (their own homes, parents' rooms attached to nursery schools, youth clubs, etc.).

B. ISSUES FOR ANALYSIS AND THEMES FOR FURTHER WORK

A determination to take seriously the implementation of a greater role for education in local development raises many issues of general importance. The ELD Project clearly recognised a number of these from the beginning. Some of these concern major questions of national justice and equity between groups in the society. These focus attention on the possibilities, limitations and consequences of adapting education more fully to the needs of local development. These then in turn lead on to discussion of more particular issues, which in turn leads back to the general issues of objectives, values and ideologies - for it has also to be recognised that there is room for differing interpretations of all the terms involved - education, development, local, community. Each of these of necessity involves different images, different perceptions and different allocations of value and desirability. Choices have to be made; not all objectives can be filled at once. Finance will not be available for every scheme, however promising. Consideration of these is in any event the stuff of policy-makers' lives, in education as in every other matter of major public interest.

In the present report, some of these issues have been raised specifically; others have been implicit; but together they indicate the areas in which further work in the field is necessary.

1) The first, and most important perhaps because it underlines the extent of policy commitment, revolves around the need to balance the interests of all the parties concerned. Education in OECD countries has always been justified principally in terms of its benefits to individuals and second in terms of its benefits to

the nation, principally in the sphere of economic development. Giving it a focus on individuals as members of local communities gives it a legitimation in unfamiliar terms and immediately raises a number of important questions:

- the extent to which education should be turned towards local development;

- ways to resolve conflicts of interest between national and local aims;

- ways to ensure that individuals benefit to the maximum as individuals where community needs are also high as is the case in the kinds of areas we are discussing;

- the criteria for choosing educational priorities of this kind, especially in an era of severe limitation on public spending;

- more generally, the value to be accorded to different conceptions of the educational endeavour at all levels and in all cycles.

These dimensions of the central question "what is education about" came very much to the fore in a project on education and local development and inevitably surround consideration of the more radical innovations described. This is notably the case in relation to the "Microsociety" experiments which go furthest in the direction of a re-ordering of the values publicly accorded to the education of small children. Here, accepted wisdom about the "higher" aims of education is most radically challenged. Further, the persistence of low levels of social mobility in spite of decades of educational reform and improvement need to be brought into the debate. The general debate about equity and equality of opportunity goes well beyond the confines of the project here reported; nevertheless, its outcomes cannot fail to be of particular salience to the discussion of education and local development.

2) Finance, organisation and governance issues have been beyond the purview of the present report. It is clear, however, that many aspects of existing education structures and systems will be altered - in many cases quite radically - by a re-orientation of the institutions concerned towards a greater role in local development. Bringing that change into being; persuading all concerned not only to accept the consequences but to be actively and positively involved; raising the monies necessary for experimentation on a sufficient scale and over a sufficiently long period of time; providing training and retraining facilities - all these involve important questions of who is to be involved, where action is to be initiated, by whom changes are to be carried out, how new arrangements are to be created and maintained, how necessary co-ordination is to be ensured.

These questions are difficult and it would seem most appropriate to keep the answers as closely related to concrete strategies as possible. Much of the work in similar areas has concentrated too much on questions concerning the "how" of the issues in the abstract; it is suggested that here the emphasis be on the ways in which countries are at present doing things in this domain. Here, as in other presentations of the projects in the present report, the emphasis should be on actual cases, on innovatory strategies in practice, on what is actually working, in short, on success on the ground. It is, therefore, important to proceed with case studies.

Such an approach requires evaluation by people closely concerned. One presently being used in the United States is that of small groups of people each closely involved in a particular innovatory practice in the appropriate field visiting, learning about and evaluating others of a similar kind. In this way, the relevance of any aspect of an experiment to the needs and experiences of those most closely involved on the ground and the success for them of any innovation can be assessed. This approach lends itself well to CERI field-based activities and the case study approach and, in the opinion of the national participants in the Project, CERI could provide a useful centre for the international exchange of evaluation experiences of this kind.

3) A crucial element in the success of local development policies and activities is the success of the collaboration that can be achieved between public and private and private non-profit sectors. Many schemes, especially those that concern the improvement of employment opportunities in the big cities necessarily involve co-operation between public agencies and private instances and interests. Economic regeneration can certainly not occur through public sector activities alone. Businesses, both small and large, have important roles to play. Both their needs and their potential contribution should be analysed in the framework of education and local development. Private sector organisers have both jobs and funds to offer. They also have expertise that can be harnessed for the benefit of the community. Some companies are doing this already. Such experiences of successful intermeshing of public and private interests and activities again need to be analysed so as to be transferable to other places.

4) Not least, of course, the curriculum is crucial. The content of courses or more generally of "learning experience" is linked to local development and the methods used to impart information and train in particular skills need further analysis. The curriculum, explicit and hidden, has a major socialisation function. In relation to education for local development, curricula will have many new elements. Each will need materials, each will need investigation with particular reference to the attitudes and values inculcated. New ways will have to be found of assessing competences acquired. New equilibria between subjects will have to be worked out. Staff will have to recognise that the linkages they make between subject areas and the values

they attribute to any endeavour may not be those of the students. Ways will have to be found of reconciling these differences in a common endeavour.

5) Dissemination of results. International exchange of information on concrete projects was found to be the great value of the Venice meeting. It is recommended that this should continue, the exchanges including: field-based meetings outside the OECD, case-studies and the preparation of synthesis reports of these, and in-house research on specific themes.

6) Specific themes and populations. Education for local development is, of course, a vast field and a start only has been made here to sketch its contours by citing specific activities being pursued in a number of OECD countries. These indicate both the elements for new and more appropriate policies of urban development increasingly being implemented and the role that different forms of education can play within that framework. But not all deprived urban groups share identical problems. Development is multifaceted. A next step, therefore, should be to identify and select specific issues for closer analysis. In particular, these should concern the needs of different populations - ethnic minorities and migrants, girls and women, older and marginal workers, the illiterate, the unqualified school-leavers or young worker - and certain themes not sufficiently covered in depth hitherto. These should include:

- the importance of pre-school education;

- the links between the effects of policies for rural and urban areas;

- alternative forms of enterprise appropriate in small-scale local development policies and the educational responses to them. These include production co-operatives;

- alternative forms of training, both in and out of school, such as in training co-operatives and training workshops.

C. EPILOGUE

It is hoped that the above analysis of education/local development activities will be helpful in the sense that countries seeking solutions to their own problems may see what others are doing and, possibly, build on their experiences - sometimes to reject what has unsuccessfully been attempted, sometimes to adopt or adapt what has begun to show promise.

But beyond this, the above analysis viewed as a whole gives substance to certain principles that would seem to have world-wide application. Profound as they are, they can still be stated in quite simple language:

i) The aim of any project on education and local development must be the creation of more effective ways of improving the life chances and living conditions of the millions of urban dwellers who still live in poverty. They all need help so as to be able to help themselves; they need skills and capacities; they need to learn to obtain access to facilities, to acquire a greater sense of the possible. Above all, perhaps, they need to have dignity and to acquire a greater sense of their own value.

ii) <u>Education for development must be education for all children.</u> It must not merely increase understanding by the disadvantaged of their disadvantage; it must help them to act to alter the situation not only of themselves but of others. Teaching and curricula must use and reflect the social and economic problems that surround the children in their daily lives.

iii) As a result of such a re-orientation towards education for development, children and young people should take their place in local life, and indeed national life, much better equipped to profit from their own resources, however limited, and much better able to contribute to the creation of new ones. From this the whole of society will benefit.

iv) The economically depressed national societies of the 1980s have much to gain from a resurgence of entrepreneurial activity and from the improved morale and social energies that this newly-oriented education can do so much to release. What is good for the locality, can certainly also be good for the nation as a whole.

BIBLIOGRAPHY

Actualité de la Formation Permanente (1980). "Petite entreprise et formation", N°. 45, March-April.

Alluli, G. (1980). "Education and local development: the case of Italy", paper presented to the OECD-Italian Ministry of Education meeting on "Education, urban development and local initiatives", Venice, 21-25 April.

Arclight (July 1979). Journal of the Action Resource Centre, London.

Autrement (1979). "Et si chacun créait son emploi ?", N°. 20, September. Whole issue.

Avenirs (1980). "Comment créer son entreprise", N°. 311, February.

Bethel, D. (1979). "The response of higher education: its means and methods", paper presented to an OECD Conference on "Higher education and the community", Paris, March 1980.

Birch, D. et al. (1979). The Behavioural Foundations of Neighbourhood Change, U.S. Department of Housing and Urban Development, Washington D.C.

Birch, J. (1979). The Job Generation Process, MIT, Boston, Mass.

Birmingham City Council (1979). Birmingham Inner City Partnership. Birmingham.

Birmingham Community Development Project Team (1977). Employment: Workers on the Scrapheap. Final Report, N°. 2, Birmingham Community Development Project.

Blichfeldt, J. (1975). "The relations between school and the place of work", in School and Community, CERI/OECD, Paris, pp. 70-87.

Blomqvist, K. (1980). "Swedish employee-owned firms: an emerging cooperative sector?", paper presented to an OECD meeting at Dartington Hall, 12-14 September 1980.

Boudon, R. (1973). L'inégalité des chances, A. Colin, Paris.

Brison D. (1973). "Out of school education in the social science sector", Phi Delta Kappan, December, pp. 237-239.

Brison, D. (1978). "The community involvement program", unpublished paper, Ontario Institute for Studies in Education, Toronto.

Brooks, C. (1977). "Youthaid evidence in response to the Manpower Services Commission Document: the new special programmes for unemployed people ...", London

Business Week (1978). Special Report: "Americans Change", 20 February, pp. 64-78.

Canberra Times (1981). "Technology park to be set up in Adelaide", 13.4.81, p. 2.

Carpanelli, F. (1980). "Cooperatives in Italy", paper presented to an OECD meeting at Dartington Hall, 12-14 September 1980.

CDP Intelligence Unit (1979). The National Community Development Project, Inter Project Report 1973, London.

Center for Community Economic Development (1975). Community Development Corporations, Boston, Mass.

Center for Community Economic Development (1974). "CDC Board Training Needs", Boston, Mass.

Centre for Cooperation Among World's Cities (1980). The Child and the City, Franco Angeli, Milan.

Commonwealth Secretariat (1978). Youth in Business. Report on a Commonwealth Regional Seminar.

Comune di Venezia, Assessorato alla Pubblica Istruzione (no date). Citta-Scuola-Citta, Itinerari Educativi. Whole series, e.g. L'artigianato.

Comune di Venezia, Istituto per il Lavoro (1980). "Education et expansion urbaine", unpublished document.

Corporation for Public-Private Ventures (no date). "The youth entrepreneurship initiative", Philadelphia.

Council of Europe (1978). Renewing Europe's Inner Cities, European Regional Planning Study Series, N°. 9, Strasbourg.

Council of the Great City Schools (1977). "A national urban education policy", first draft.

Curriculum Development Centre (1980). Core Curriculum for Australian Schools, Canberra.

Davis, R. (1978a). "Small business and employment creation in Calcutta: the CYSEC case", paper prepared for USAID.

Davis, R. (1978b). "Planning education for employment", Center for Studies in Education and Development, Harvard Graduate School of Education, Cambridge, Mass.

Delors, J. (1978). *La création d'emplois dans le secteur tertiaire ; le troisième secteur en France*. Programme de Recherche et d'Action sur l'Evolution du Marché de l'Emploi, Commission des Communautés Européennes, Brussels.

Dun and Bradstreet, in Birch, D., *et al*. (1979).

Department of Education and Science, London (1980). Country Report on Education and Local Development in the United Kindom.

Department of the Environment (1970 and 1978). Inner Area Study Birmingham. "Educational Action Projects", Vols. 1 and 2. Reports by the Consultants, London. Vol. I IAS/B/13, Vol. II is IAS/B/14 and Vol. III IAS/B/24.

Department of the Environment (1974). *Inner Area Study Lambeth: Schools Project*. IAS/LA/13.

Department of the Environment (1978a). Inner Cities Directorate, *Report on Inner City Policy*, September-October, N°. 7, London.

Department of the Environment (1978b). *Final Report of the Working Party on Environmental Education*, London. Ref. EB(78)39.

Department of Industrial Affairs and Employment, South Australia (1980). "City projects for unemployed youth", brochure, Adelaide.

Dickinson, R.E. (1967). *The City Region in Western Europe*, Routledge and Kegan Paul, Ltd., London.

Doe, B. (1980). "Children learn more by teaching their juniors", *Times Educational Supplement*, N°. 3328, 21.3.1980.

Drewett, R. (1979). "Urbanization Trends in Selected OECD Countries". A paper prepared for the OECD (out of print).

Edel, M. (1970). "Development or dispersal? Approaches to ghetto poverty", Center for Community Economic Development, Boston, Mass.

Falk, N. (no date). "First steps in regenerating London's inner areas", London Looks Forward, Conference Paper N°. 6, London.

Field, F., ed. (1977). *Education and the Urban Crisis*, Routledge and Kegan Paul, London.

Filkin, F., Yarnit, M. (1980). "When a second chance is a fine thing", *Times Higher Education Supplement*, N°. 383, 22.8.80, p. 11.

Fisk, E. (1978). "Programs for adults bypassing neediest", Learning, Vol. I, N°. 4, Spring, p. 16.

Fish, J. (1973). Black Power, White Control, Princeton University Press, Princeton.

Furst, L. (1979). "Work: an educational alternative to schooling", The Urban Review, Vol. 11, N°. 3, Fall, pp. 149-157.

Gill, O. (1977). Luke Street, Macmillan, London.

Gleaser, E. (1979). "The community college in the United States", paper presented to an OECD Conference on "Higher education and the community", Paris, February 1980.

Goodman, R. (1973). After the Planners, Simon and Schuster, New York.

Gorb, P. (1978a). "Management development for the small firm", Personnel Management, Vol. 10, N°. 1, January, pp. 24-27.

Gorb, P. (1978b). "Is this the key to urban renewal?", Small Business Guardian, 28.7.78.

Haberer, P., Vonk, F. (1978). Urban Revitalization, Johns Hopkins University Press, Baltimore.

Hamilton, M. (1980). "On creating viable work experience programs: design and implementation", Youthwork National Policy Study, Occasional paper N°. 3, Cornell University, Ithaca.

Harvey, B. (1980). "L.e.a. versus community", Times Higher Education Supplement, 17.10.80. p. 4.

Herzlich, G. (1978). "Le chômage des jeunes diplômés", Le Monde de l'Education, N°. 44, November, pp. 7-27.

Holloway, W. (1980). "Youth participation: a strategy to increase the role of in-school youth in creating job opportunities", Youthwork National Policy Study, Occasional Paper N°. 4, Cornell University, Ithaca.

IBM-URBED (1977). Creating Work Through Small Enterprise, London.

Jackson, in OECD (1980a).

Jencks, C. (1972). Inequality: a Reassessment of Family and Schooling in America, New York.

Jones, P. (1978). Community Education in Practice: a Review, Social Evaluation Unit, Oxford.

Laplume, Y. (1979). "Les collectivités locales et l'université en France : image, attentes et besoins", paper presented to an OECD Conference on "Higher education and the community", Paris, February 1980.

Le Monde (1979). "L'Année Economique et Sociale", Paris.

Levin, H. (1979). "Economic democracy, education and social change", Program Report N°. 79-B16, Center for Educational Research, Stanford University .

Littlewood, B. (1980). "Case study: the North East London Polytechnic Company Limited", paper prepared for the OECD/CERI.

Mackay, S. (1979). "Do-it-yourself the community way", Community Care, November.

Maguire, P. (1979). "Teach the public to teach the planners", Building Design, 2.3.1979, pp. 12-13.

McKie, R. (1980a). "The rise of the teaching company", Times Higher Education Supplement, 29.2.80, p. 9.

McKie, R. (1980b). "Microchip first for Edinburgh", Times Higher Education Supplement, N°. 403, p. 8.

Minister for Employment and Immigration, Ottawa (1980). Press release on LEDA (Local Economic Development Assistance) Program.

Ministry of Education, Sweden (1980). "Sweden: a case study of the university college of Lulea", paper presented to an OECD Conference on "Higher education and the community", Paris, February 1980.

Ministry of Labour, Ministry of Education, Denmark (1978). "Measures to combat youth unemployment taken according to the employment plan", Second edition, Copenhagen.

Molle, W., Botterweg, T. (1978). "Le comportement des entrepreneurs : Pays-Bas", paper presented to the conference of the Association Internationale pour la Statistique Régionale et Urbaine, Reims.

National Commission on Resources for Youth (1974). New roles for Youth, Citation Press, New York.

National Commission on Resources for Youth (1975). Youth Participation: Report to HEW.

National Times (Australia) (1981). "The real price of the cheapest land", 29/3-4/4, p. 15.

National Training Council (1981). Small Business Education and Training in Australia, Canberra.

Netherlands Scientific Council for Government Policy (1977). "Do we make work our business?". Reports to the Government, Nº. 13, 1978. The Hague.

OECD Ad Hoc Group on Urban Decline (1980a). "Urban Decline: an overview of the issues in OECD countries".

OECD (1980b). Youth Unemployment: The Causes and Consequences, Paris.

Orefice, P. (1978). "MOTER" - a territorial model for educational programming, theoretical guidelines and working outlines, also in Italian and French, University of Naples, Istituto di pedagogia e filosofia morale, Naples.

Orefice, P. (1979) "The cultural self-awareness of a local community - an experience in the south of Italy", paper presented to the ninth Conference of the Comparative Education Society in Europe, Valencia, 25-29 June.

Pena, J. et al. (1979). "Youth opportunity program: training for the future, manpower for today", The Urban Review, Vol. 11, Nº. 4, winter.

Pepper, B. (1978). "Urban role of Saskatchewan community colleges", Learning, Vol. 1, Nº. 4, spring.

Perry, S. (1978). Building a Model Black Community: The Roxbury Action Program, Center for Community Economic Development, Boston, Mass.

Pflaumer, H. (1967). "Problems of Inner Areas", in The City Region in Western Europe, Routledge and Kegan Paul, Ltd., London.

Raynor, J., Harden, J. (1973). Cities, Communities and the Young - Readings in Urban Education, Vol. I, Routledge and Kegan Paul, London.

Richmond, G. (1975). "The Society School: students organise a model of society in school", in Talbot N. (ed.), Raising Children in Modern Urban America, Little, Brown & Co., New York.

Rist, R. (1979). "On the education of guest-worker children in Germany", School Review, Vol. 87, Nº. 3, May, pp. 243-273.

Rutter, M. et al. (1979). Fifteen Thousand Hours, Harvard University Press, Boston, Mass.

Schonleber, J. (1980). "Community colleges and community development", *Community and Junior College Journal*, March, pp. 4-8.

Schools Commission (1980). *Schooling for 15 and 16 Year Olds*, Canberra.

Schools Commission (1981). *Report for the Triennium 1982-1984*, Canberra.

Schools Council (1979). "The Schools Council Industry Project", London.

Sheils, M. et al. (1977). "City schools in crisis", *Newsweek*, 12.9.1977, pp. 62-70.

Sher, J. and OECD (1981). *Rural Education in Urbanized Nations: Issues and Innovations*, Westview Press, Boulder, Colorado.

Short, C., Levine, J. (1979). "The neglected resource: the use of employment and training programs in economic development strategy", Northeast-Midwest Institute, Washington D.C.

Smith, G. (1977). "Positive discrimination by area in education: the EPA idea re-examined", *Oxford Review of Education*, Vol. 3, N°. 3, pp. 269-281.

Spikins, J. (1980). "Case study: Loughborough Consultants Limited", paper prepared for the OECD/CERI.

Taylor, K. (1980). "Current technological developments", paper presented to an OECD/PEB meeting at Lochem, Holland, 6-10 October 1980.

Times Higher Education Supplement (1980a). "Colleges help revive inner city area", N°. 386, 14.3.80, p. 2.

Times Higher Education Supplement (1980b). "Deal to boost urban development is signed", N°. 386, 14.3.80, p. 5.

Times Higher Education Supplement (1980c). "Why polytechnics must keep a strong local connection", 29.2.80, p. 27.

The Times (1980). "Design 'should be central part of child's education'", 10.9./80, p 6.

Times Educational Supplement (1980). "The science of recycling the unemployed", N°. 3325, 29.2.80, p. 4.

Topping, P., Smith, G. (1977). *Government against poverty? Liverpool Community Development Project, 1970-75*. Oxford.

Urbed (no date). *Employment and the Small Farm*, Social and Community Planning Research, London.

Urbed (1978a). *Ensuring a Future for Small Enterprise in Covent Garden*, London.

Urbed (1978b). *Linking the College and the Community: Centres of Knowledge and Economic Development*, Urbed Research Trust, London.

Urbed (1978c). *Linking the College and the Community: Fostering New Enterprises*, Urbed Research Trust, London.

Urbed (1980). *Linking the College and the Community: A Practical Guide*, London.

U.S. Department of Commerce, Office of Minority Business Enterprise (1974). "Report of the task force on education and training for minority business enterprise", Washington D.C.

U.S. Department of Housing and Urban Development (no date). *Methods of Impact Analysis, Vol. 2, Netighbourhood Self-Help Development*.

U.S. Department of Housing and Urban Development (1979). *Occasional Papers in Housing and Community Affairs*, Nº. 4.

U.S. Department of Housing and Urban Development, U.S. Department of Commerce (1979a). *Economic Development: New Roles for City Government*, Washington D.C.

U.S. Department of Housing and Urban Development, U.S. Department of Commerce (1979b). *Local Economic Development: Tools and Techniques*, Washington D.C.

U.S. Department of Housing and Urban Development, U.S. Department of Commerce (1979c). *Neighborhood Self-Help Development*, Washington D.C.

U.S. Department of Labor (1979). *Youth*, Washington D.C.

Usher, B. (1977). *Etobicoke Community Involvement Program Evaluation*. Ontario Ministry of Education, Toronto.

U.S. Office of Education (no date). "Instructional strategies in schools with high concentrations of low income pupils", Report of the National Task Forces on Urban Education, Rural and Migrant Education, Native American Education, Bilingual/Bicultural Education, Washington D.C.

Weiler, H. (1978). "Education and development: from the age of innocence to the age of scepticism", *Comparative Education*, Vol. 13, Nº. 3, October, pp. 179-197.

Wolman, H., Mueller, U. (1979). *Urban Decline: Its Extent, Causes and Consequences in OECD Countries*, The Urban Institute, Washington D.C.

Youthaid (1978a). *Further Education Curriculum Alternatives for Areas of High and Prolonged Youth Unemployment*, London.

Youthaid (1978b). *The Youth Opportunities Programme: Making it Work*, London.

Youthwork Inc. (1979). *Youthwork, an Overview*, Washington D.C.

OECD SALES AGENTS
DÉPOSITAIRES DES PUBLICATIONS DE L'OCDE

ARGENTINA – ARGENTINE
Carlos Hirsch S.R.L., Florida 165, 4° Piso (Galería Guemes)
1333 BUENOS AIRES, Tel. 33.1787.2391 y 30.7122

AUSTRALIA – AUSTRALIE
Australia and New Zealand Book Company Pty, Ltd.,
10 Aquatic Drive, Frenchs Forest, N.S.W. 2086
P.O. Box 459, BROOKVALE, N.S.W. 2100

AUSTRIA – AUTRICHE
OECD Publications and Information Center
4 Simrockstrasse 5300 BONN. Tel. (0228) 21.60.45
Local Agent/Agent local :
Gerold and Co., Graben 31, WIEN 1. Tel. 52.22.35

BELGIUM – BELGIQUE
Jean De Lannoy, Service Publications OCDE
avenue du Roi 202, B-1060 BRUXELLES. Tel. 02/538.51.69

BRAZIL – BRÉSIL
Mestre Jou S.A., Rua Guaipa 518,
Caixa Postal 24090, 05089 SAO PAULO 10. Tel. 261.1920
Rua Senador Dantas 19 s/205-6, RIO DE JANEIRO GB.
Tel. 232.07.32

CANADA
Renouf Publishing Company Limited,
2182 ouest, rue Ste-Catherine,
MONTRÉAL, Qué. H3H 1M7. Tel. (514)937.3519
OTTAWA, Ont. K1P 5A6, 61 Sparks Street

DENMARK – DANEMARK
Munksgaard Export and Subscription Service
35, Nørre Søgade
DK 1370 KØBENHAVN K. Tel. +45.1.12.85.70

FINLAND – FINLANDE
Akateeminen Kirjakauppa
Keskuskatu 1, 00100 HELSINKI 10. Tel. 65.11.22

FRANCE
Bureau des Publications de l'OCDE,
2 rue André-Pascal, 75775 PARIS CEDEX 16. Tel. (1) 524.81.67
Principal correspondant :
13602 AIX-EN-PROVENCE : Librairie de l'Université.
Tel. 26.18.08

GERMANY – ALLEMAGNE
OECD Publications and Information Center
4 Simrockstrasse 5300 BONN. Tel. (0228) 21.60.45

GREECE – GRÈCE
Librairie Kauffmann, 28 rue du Stade,
ATHÈNES 132. Tel. 322.21.60

HONG-KONG
Government Information Services,
Publications/Sales Section, Baskerville House,
2/F., 22 Ice House Street

ICELAND – ISLANDE
Snaebjörn Jónsson and Co., h.f.,
Hafnarstraeti 4 and 9, P.O.B. 1131, REYKJAVIK.
Tel. 13133/14281/11936

INDIA – INDE
Oxford Book and Stationery Co. :
NEW DELHI-1, Scindia House. Tel. 45896
CALCUTTA 700016, 17 Park Street. Tel. 240832

INDONESIA – INDONÉSIE
PDIN-LIPI, P.O. Box 3065/JKT., JAKARTA, Tel. 583467

IRELAND – IRLANDE
TDC Publishers – Library Suppliers
12 North Frederick Street, DUBLIN 1 Tel. 744835-749677

ITALY – ITALIE
Libreria Commissionaria Sansoni :
Via Lamarmora 45, 50121 FIRENZE. Tel. 579751/584468
Via Bartolini 29, 20155 MILANO. Tel. 365083
Sub-depositari :
Ugo Tassi
Via A. Farnese 28, 00192 ROMA. Tel. 310590
Editrice e Libreria Herder,
Piazza Montecitorio 120, 00186 ROMA. Tel. 6794628
Costantino Ercolano, Via Generale Orsini 46, 80132 NAPOLI. Tel. 405210
Libreria Hoepli, Via Hoepli 5, 20121 MILANO. Tel. 865446
Libreria Scientifica, Dott. Lucio de Biasio "Aeiou"
Via Meravigli 16, 20123 MILANO Tel. 807679
Libreria Zanichelli
Piazza Galvani 1/A, 40124 Bologna Tel. 237389
Libreria Lattes, Via Garibaldi 3, 10122 TORINO. Tel. 519274
La diffusione delle edizioni OCSE è inoltre assicurata dalle migliori librerie nelle città più importanti.

JAPAN – JAPON
OECD Publications and Information Center,
Landic Akasaka Bldg., 2-3-4 Akasaka,
Minato-ku, TOKYO 107 Tel. 586.2016

KOREA – CORÉE
Pan Korea Book Corporation,
P.O. Box n° 101 Kwangwhamun, SÉOUL. Tel. 72.7369

LEBANON – LIBAN
Documenta Scientifica/Redico,
Edison Building, Bliss Street, P.O. Box 5641, BEIRUT.
Tel. 354429 – 344425

MALAYSIA – MALAISIE
University of Malaya Co-operative Bookshop Ltd.
P.O. Box 1127, Jalan Pantai Baru
KUALA LUMPUR. Tel. 51425, 54058, 54361

THE NETHERLANDS – PAYS-BAS
Staatsuitgeverij, Verzendboekhandel,
Chr. Plantijnstraat 1 Postbus 20014
2500 EA S-GRAVENHAGE. Tel. nr. 070.789911
Voor bestellingen: Tel. 070.789208

NEW ZEALAND – NOUVELLE-ZÉLANDE
Publications Section,
Government Printing Office Bookshops:
AUCKLAND: Retail Bookshop: 25 Rutland Street,
Mail Orders: 85 Beach Road, Private Bag C.P.O.
HAMILTON: Retail Ward Street,
Mail Orders, P.O. Box 857
WELLINGTON: Retail: Mulgrave Street (Head Office),
Cubacade World Trade Centre
Mail Orders: Private Bag
CHRISTCHURCH: Retail: 159 Hereford Street,
Mail Orders: Private Bag
DUNEDIN: Retail: Princes Street
Mail Order: P.O. Box 1104

NORWAY – NORVÈGE
J.G. TANUM A/S Karl Johansgate 43
P.O. Box 1177 Sentrum OSLO 1. Tel. (02) 80.12.60

PAKISTAN
Mirza Book Agency, 65 Shahrah Quaid-E-Azam, LAHORE 3.
Tel. 66839

PHILIPPINES
National Book Store, Inc.
Library Services Division, P.O. Box 1934, MANILA.
Tel. Nos. 49.43.06 to 09, 40.53.45, 49.45.12

PORTUGAL
Livraria Portugal, Rua do Carmo 70-74,
1117 LISBOA CODEX. Tel. 360582/3

SINGAPORE – SINGAPOUR
Information Publications Pte Ltd,
Pei-Fu Industrial Building,
24 New Industrial Road N° 02-06
SINGAPORE 1953, Tel. 2831786, 2831798

SPAIN – ESPAGNE
Mundi-Prensa Libros, S.A.
Castelló 37, Apartado 1223, MADRID-1. Tel. 275.46.55
Libreria Bosch, Ronda Universidad 11, BARCELONA 7.
Tel. 317.53.08, 317.53.58

SWEDEN – SUÈDE
AB CE Fritzes Kungl Hovbokhandel,
Box 16 356, S 103 27 STH, Regeringsgatan 12,
DS STOCKHOLM. Tel. 08/23.89.00
Subscription Agency/Abonnements:
Wennergren-Williams AB,
Box 13004, S104 25 STOCKHOLM.
Tel. 08/54.12.00

SWITZERLAND – SUISSE
OECD Publications and Information Center
4 Simrockstrasse 5300 BONN. Tel. (0228) 21.60.45
Local Agents/Agents locaux
Librairie Payot, 6 rue Grenus, 1211 GENÈVE 11. Tel. 022.31.89.50

TAIWAN – FORMOSE
Good Faith Worldwide Int'l Co., Ltd.
9th floor, No. 118, Sec. 2,
Chung Hsiao E. Road
TAIPEI. Tel. 391.7396/391.7397

THAILAND – THAILANDE
Suksit Siam Co., Ltd., 1715 Rama IV Rd,
Samyan, BANGKOK 5. Tel. 2511630

TURKEY – TURQUIE
Kültur Yayinlari Is-Türk Ltd. Sti.
Atatürk Bulvari N° : 77/B
KIZILAY/ANKARA. Tel. 17 02 66
Dolmabahce Cad. No : 29
BESIKTAS/ISTANBUL. Tel. 60 71 88

UNITED KINGDOM – ROYAUME-UNI
H.M. Stationery Office, P.O.B. 276,
LONDON SW8 5DT. Tel. (01) 622.3316, or
49 High Holborn, LONDON WC1V 6 HB (personal callers)
Branches at: EDINBURGH, BIRMINGHAM, BRISTOL,
MANCHESTER, BELFAST.

UNITED STATES OF AMERICA – ÉTATS-UNIS
OECD Publications and Information Center, Suite 1207,
1750 Pennsylvania Ave., N.W. WASHINGTON, D.C.20006 – 4582
Tel. (202) 724.1857

VENEZUELA
Libreria del Este, Avda. F. Miranda 52, Edificio Galipan,
CARACAS 106. Tel. 32.23.01/33.26.04/31.58.38

YUGOSLAVIA – YOUGOSLAVIE
Jugoslovenska Knjiga, Knez Mihajlova 2, P.O.B. 36, BEOGRAD.
Tel. 621.992

Les commandes provenant de pays où l'OCDE n'a pas encore désigné de dépositaire peuvent être adressées à :
OCDE, Bureau des Publications, 2, rue André-Pascal, 75775 PARIS CEDEX 16.
Orders and inquiries from countries where sales agents have not yet been appointed may be sent to:
OECD, Publications Office, 2, rue André-Pascal, 75775 PARIS CEDEX 16.

67048-10-1983

OECD PUBLICATIONS, 2, rue André-Pascal, 75775 PARIS CEDEX 16 - No. 42809 1983
PRINTED IN FRANCE
(96 84 01 1) ISBN 92-64-12536-1